Think You're Crazy? Think Again

Anthony P. Morrison is a Professor of Clinical Psychology at the University of Manchester and Associate Director for Early Intervention Services at Bolton, Salford and Trafford Mental Health Trust.

Julia C. Renton is a Consultant Clinical Psychologist at Bedfordshire and Luton Mental Health and Social Care Partnership Trust.

Paul French is a research cognitive therapist at the University of Manchester and Associate Director for Early Intervention Services at Bolton, Salford and Trafford Mental Health Trust.

Richard P. Bentall is a Professor of Clinical Psychology at the University of Bangor

Are you troubled by hearing voices or seeing visions that others do not? Do you believe that other people are trying to harm you or control you? Do you feel that something odd is going on that you can't explain or that things are happening around you with a special meaning? Do you worry that other people can read your mind or that thoughts are being put in your head?

Think you're crazy? Think again provides an effective step-by-step aid to understanding your problems, making positive changes and promoting recovery. Written by experts in the field, this book will help you to:

- understand how your problems developed and what keeps them going
- use questionnaires and monitoring sheets to identify and track changes in the links between your experiences, how you make sense of these and how you feel and behave
- learn how to change thoughts, feelings and behaviour for the better
- practise skills between sessions using worksheets

Based on clinically proven techniques and filled with examples of how cognitive therapy can help people with distressing psychotic experiences, *Think you're crazy? Think again* will be a valuable resource for people with psychosis.

Think You're Crazy? Think Again

A Resource Book for Cognitive Therapy for Psychosis

ANTHONY P. MORRISON, JULIA C. RENTON, PAUL FRENCH, RICHARD P. BENTALL

Routledge
Taylor & Francis Group

LONDON AND NEW YORK

First published 2008 by Routledge
27 Church Road, Hove, East Sussex BN3 2FA

Simultaneously published in the USA and Canada
by Routledge
270 Madison Avenue, New York NY 10016

Reprinted 2009, 2010 and 2011

Routledge is an imprint of the Taylor & Francis Group, an Informa business

© 2008 Anthony P. Morrison, Julia C. Renton, Paul French,
Richard P. Bentall

Typeset in Stone Serif by Garfield Morgan, Swansea, West Glamorgan
Printed and bound in Great Britain by TJ International Ltd, Padstow, Cornwall
Paperback cover design by Sandra Heath

British Library Cataloguing in Publication Data
A catalogue record for this book is available from the British Library

Library of Congress Cataloging-in-Publication Data
Think you're crazy? think again : a resource book for cognitive therapy
for psychosis / Anthony P. Morrison . . . [et al.].
        p. cm.
    Includes bibliographical references and index.
    ISBN 978-1-58391-836-4 (hardback) – ISBN 978-1-58391-837-1 (pbk.)
1. Psychoses–Treatment. 2. Cognitive therapy. I. Morrison, Anthony P.,
1969-
    RC512.T53 2008
    616.89'142–dc22
                                                          2007037963

ISBN: 978-1-58391-836-4 (hbk)
ISBN: 978-1-58391-837-1 (pbk)

Dedications

To Soph and Lula, for their massive contribution to my own
well-being – AM
To Lawrie, Thomas and Oliver, with love and thanks – JR
To Delia, Chloe, Nadia and Ben, with big love – PF
To Aisling, Keeva and Fintan – RB

Contents

Acknowledgements and an introductory note

Much of this book owes a great deal to the work of many clinicians and researchers. In particular, we would like to thank Tim Beck for developing cognitive therapy in the first place, and Dennis Greenberger and Christine Padesky for writing *Mind Over Mood*, which is such a useful tool for cognitive therapists and patients alike, and certainly inspired this book. We would also like to thank our colleagues in the field of cognitive therapy and psychosis, who are far too numerous to mention. Finally, we would like to thank our service users and their families for providing us with lots of feedback over the years about the best ways in which we can make our approach accessible. We hope that this book does justice to their help, and makes cognitive therapy more accessible to people with distressing psychotic experiences. It is not intended as a self-help book, but rather as a tool that will assist people when they are receiving cognitive therapy from a suitably trained mental health professional. That is not to say that this book is not to be read by interested people who aren't in therapy – simply that it is likely to be of most use when there is someone to advise and guide you through its chapters.

What is psychosis?

Calvin is a 26-year-old man. Since the age of 18 he has heard voices that nobody else can hear, often when nobody else is around. Mostly they seem to come from nearby on his left, but sometimes it seems as if they originate from a point just behind his forehead. They can happen at all times of day, but most often in the late afternoon or evening. Sometimes, as many as ten days can pass without him hearing the voices, but at other times they torment him for hours on end. They also vary in loudness and clarity, at times becoming a low mumble that he can hardly make out and at other times speaking as clearly as someone standing right next to him. He has considered various explanations for them. Sometimes he blames them on God or the Devil. At other times (usually after one of his regular meetings with his psychiatrist or community psychiatric nurse) he tries to accept that there is something wrong in his brain, although he never finds this explanation completely convincing. On the advice of his doctor, he has tried to ignore them, but he often finds this impossible. When they are particularly distressing he tries to cope with them by returning to his flat, lying down on his bed, putting on his headphones and listening to loud music.

The voices did not always make him so upset. When they first began, they were actually quite comforting. They spoke to him about the terrible time in his childhood when he had been sexually abused, telling him that he had not been at fault and that he had nothing to be ashamed of. Vaguely aware that this experience was very unusual, he kept it to himself. The voices would appear when he was feeling especially unhappy and would cheer him up. However, everything changed when, aged 22, Calvin had a fight with an employer, who picked on him with racist abuse. Finally snapping after months of torment, Calvin had lashed out and hit him and the employer had called the police. When interviewed, he had (foolishly it now seems) talked openly about the voices for the first time, telling a police surgeon who had been called to the police station to examine him. As a consequence, he was 'sectioned' (involuntarily detained in hospital) under Section 22 of the Mental Health Act, and was forced to receive antipsychotic medication for the first time. It had been an awful experience. After he initially refused to take the drugs, the nurses held him down and painfully injected him in his buttock. The incident was very traumatic and had reminded him of some of his earlier experiences, especially the violence and abuse he had suffered when living in a children's home.

After his stay in hospital, Calvin's voices became more and more critical. Now they often talk about him negatively, or criticize him directly. He has taken his medication on and off for the past few years. However, due to frequent visits from his community psychiatric nurse (CPN), he has been taking his drugs fairly consistently for the past few months. He has mixed feelings about the treatment, partly because he is not entirely sure that he wants the voices to go away (oddly, he often feels bored and lonely after long periods without them) and also because, when taking the drugs, he feels very lethargic, unmotivated and emotionally flat.

To many users of psychiatric services, their families and the mental health professionals who look after them, Calvin's experiences will seem very familiar. Despite this familiarity, they may also seem baffling evidence of a mind that has lost touch with reality. It is quite common for people who experience voices to feel threatened by them, and frightened that they are on a slippery slope that can only end in complete insanity. Indeed, Calvin has at times wondered whether he is slowly deteriorating and has compared himself to an elderly uncle who, some years ago, he watched slowly drift into dementia and eventually die. Calvin's friends and relatives are also frightened about what will happen to him in the future. His mother, in particular, is worried that he may become violent and uncontrollable; she regularly watches the television news and has seen many reports of psychiatric patients attacking other people, sometimes even murdering complete strangers.

The psychiatric staff who have looked after Calvin over the years have not always been helpful in this respect. Several of the psychiatrists he has seen have told him that he suffers from 'schizophrenia', and another has told him that he has a 'paranoid psychosis', but they have neglected to explain what these terms mean. The fact that the different psychiatrists do not seem to have been in complete agreement with each other has fuelled his doubts about the treatment they have offered him. To make matters more confusing, Calvin is aware that other people who have been given the same diagnoses seem to have problems that are quite different to his.

Cath is a 41-year-old woman with two grown-up children, and has been in contact with psychiatric services for more than half her lifetime. Her difficulties began 22 years ago, just after the birth of her first child, Steven, when she started to believe that social services were spying on her. Fearing that they planned to take her son away from her, she refused to leave her house. Eventually, her fear receded and two years later she gave birth to a second child, her daughter Claire.

Following the second birth, all of Cath's fears returned and became more severe than ever. Convinced that social workers were spying on her through her windows, and even watching her through her television set, she closed her curtains and refused to go outside, in case her children were snatched away from her. She even refused to answer the telephone. When a district nurse came to check on the children and was refused entry to the house, a psychiatrist was called out and Cath was eventually admitted to a psychiatric ward. Not surprisingly, perhaps, this experience only reinforced Cath's fears, and no amount of reassurance from her husband (who was able to look after the children on his own) or the nurses on the ward seemed to help.

Cath's difficulties have continued over the years and she now believes that the police are working with the local social services department to plan her prosecution. She believes that they let themselves into her house on the rare occasions that she goes out, and rearranges items such as ornaments and small pieces of furniture in order to remind her that they are watching her. On the few occasions that she does go out, Cath keeps her head down, looks at the pavement and counts in her head, in order to prevent police officers and social workers from reading her mind.

After more than two decades of these difficulties, Cath's relationship with her husband is at an all time low. He frequently reminds her that she was an inadequate mother and that he had to carry the burden of raising the children. He also tells her that she should be very grateful to him for marrying her in the first place (the marriage took place in a hurry, following the discovery that Cath was pregnant). As if to confirm his low opinion of her, Steven and Claire make very little attempt to hide how difficult they find it to see her, and visit at most once a month, despite the fact that they live in the same town.

Like Calvin, Cath has received various diagnoses, including 'puerperal psychosis' (the diagnosis she was given just after Steven was born), 'psychotic depression' and 'paranoid schizophrenia'. She is even less persuaded than Calvin that the psychiatric staff really understand what has happened to her, and the lack of a convincing explanation of her difficulties has encouraged her continuing belief that she is the victim of some kind of conspiracy.

WHAT IS PSYCHOSIS?

Many labels (for example 'schizophrenia', 'paranoia' and 'psychosis') have been used to describe the kinds of problems suffered by Calvin, Cath and the millions of other people in the world who are like them. One problem for many people who receive psychiatric care is that there is no readily accessible source of information from which they can obtain an explanation of these terms, or an account of what they might expect from their psychiatric treatment. Although there are some useful sites on the internet, most are difficult to read and different sites sometimes seem to contradict each other. There are very few books available that provide clearly presented information about mental illness. If they are lucky, patients may find a psychiatrist, psychologist or psychiatric nurse who will spend some time talking to them about their experiences, but over-stretched psychiatric services do not always provide this kind of help. This is one reason why we have written this book.

It might help if we begin by noting that the different labels that mental health professionals use when talking about their patients' difficulties have evolved historically, as different psychiatrists and psychologists have struggled to find ways of describing their patients' symptoms. Therefore, when mental health professionals use different terms – for example, when one nurse talks about a patient suffering from 'psychosis' and the other talks about the same patient suffering from 'schizophrenia' – there is usually no disagreement meant. One professional simply prefers to use a different term than the other. It is therefore important not to get too worried about the *words* used when psychiatrists, psychologists and nurses talk about their patients (although professionals may disagree about the *causes* of patients' difficulties, as we will discuss later in the book).

The broadest term used to describe the kinds of problems experienced by Calvin and Cath is *psychosis* (or 'psychotic disorder'). Psychosis simply means, roughly, a type of problem in which the patient appears to be, at least to some degree, out of touch with reality. The patient may be judged to be out of touch with reality because he or she has unusual perceptions (for example, hearing voices, as in the case of Calvin) and/or because he or she has beliefs that seem strange and unjustified to other people (most often, the terrifying belief that there is some kind of malevolent conspiracy afoot, as in the case of Cath). Patients with psychosis may also suffer from other emotional difficulties (for example, they may have difficulty coping with the demands of life, or may be very depressed). They also commonly experience changes in the way that they perceive themselves and the world around them, becoming preoccupied with unusual ideas and may withdraw as a result. However, it is the unusual experiences and beliefs that usually lead the patient to be described as psychotic.

At this point it will be useful to introduce two words that mental health professionals use to describe the main symptoms of psychosis. Calvin experienced voices of people who were not actually present. This type of experience, which (we will see later on) is surprisingly common, is known as a *hallucination*. The most common type of hallucination is auditory-verbal, like Calvin's. However, less commonly people also experience visual hallucinations (seeing things that are not really there, as in the case of a young man who believed that he could see the Devil), tactile hallucinations (for example, the sense of being touched when no one else is present) and olfactory hallucinations (smells that no one else can detect).

The term *delusion* is used by psychiatrists and psychologists to describe beliefs that are strongly held, even in the face of significant evidence against it, and which appear unbelievable or even bizarre and ridiculous to nearly everyone else. The most common type of delusion is *paranoid* or *persecutory*. People with these kinds of beliefs, for example Cath, fear that there is some kind of conspiracy against them. However, other kinds of unusual beliefs also lead people to seek psychiatric help; for example, they may believe that they have supernatural powers or enormous wealth (causing them to do things that they later regret) or feel that they are guilty of impossible crimes. An important point that we would like to make here is that, in general, people do not pick unusual beliefs out of the blue. Usually, people who have beliefs that seem bizarre or implausible to other people have good reasons for holding those beliefs. Of course, this is not to say that those beliefs accurately reflect what is happening.

DOES DIAGNOSIS MATTER?

Although there is general agreement amongst mental health professionals about the broad term 'psychosis', matters become a bit more complicated when more specific diagnostic labels are used. Despite attempts by psychiatrists and psychologists to define diagnoses precisely (for example, by writing manuals that try to define the symptoms associated with each diagnosis), there remains disagreement about how many different kinds of psychiatric disorders there are, and how they should be labelled.

One term that is often used to describe psychotic conditions is *schizophrenia*. Usually, the person who is diagnosed as suffering from schizophrenia has hallucinations and/or delusions, but also has other difficulties. For example, he or she may lack motivation, feel emotionally flat and may avoid contact with other people as much as possible. He or she may also have difficulty speaking clearly, especially when emotionally distressed. Although people diagnosed as suffering from schizophrenia are often very unhappy, this diagnosis is usually not given when the *main* problem is experienced by the person is one of mood (feelings).

If mood problems are predominant, the terms *manic depression* or *bipolar disorder* are often used (these terms mean the same thing). People who receive these diagnoses may have periods of extreme depression, and also periods of feeling *manic* (excessively high, but also irritated and panicky). However, people who are diagnosed as suffering from manic depression/bipolar disorder may also have psychotic experiences (hallucinations and delusions), especially when manic.

Because many people experience a mixture of difficulties that appear to be neither clearly schizophrenic nor clearly manic depressive, and because some psychiatrists and psychologists doubt whether these are really separate conditions, the diagnosis of *schizoaffective disorder* is often used when patients have both persisting psychotic symptoms and also persisting problems of mood.

The term *paranoia* is typically used when the person has paranoid or persecutory beliefs, and no other psychotic experiences. Many psychiatrists today prefer to use the term *delusional disorder* in these circumstances. To make matters slightly more confusing, people are sometimes diagnosed as suffering from *paranoid schizophrenia* if they have many symptoms, but paranoid fears are the most severe.

The important point for both patients and their friends and relatives to bear in mind is that diagnoses matter much less in psychiatry than in general medicine. Psychiatric diagnoses such as 'schizophrenia' and 'paranoia' do not describe completely different illnesses in the same way that 'cardiac arrest' and 'diabetes' do. Because of the disagreements that exist about diagnostic boundaries, and because patients' difficulties may change over time, it is quite common for people to be given one diagnosis at one point in time and, when another doctor comes along some months or years afterwards, a second or even third diagnosis later on.

For this reason, when helping people with psychosis, psychiatrists, psychologists and nurses should try to assess and understand the unique combination of problems experienced by each patient. Taking this approach, it is easier to understand the origins of patients' problems and, hopefully, to devise interventions that meet their needs [1].

2

Are my experiences abnormal?

In this chapter we will explain how psychotic experiences can be thought of as occurring on a continuum (range) with normal, healthy functioning [2]. We will show that there is not a clear dividing line between 'sanity' and psychiatric disorder. This observation is important because it establishes that people with psychiatric difficulties are not very different from everyone else. In fact, as we will see in later chapters, many of the difficulties experienced by people suffering from psychiatric problems can be seen as extreme variations of characteristics to which we are all prone.

As we discovered in the previous chapter, Calvin is a 26-year-old man who has heard voices since he was 18. These voices began as a positive experience, offering him support and advice. The voices started to become negative after Calvin was detained in hospital when he was 22. He was injected with medication against his wishes and he now recounts that the voices became critical and negative following this incident. At that time he was told for the first time that he suffered from schizophrenia.

HOW COMMON ARE PSYCHIATRIC DIAGNOSES LIKE SCHIZOPHRENIA?

As discussed earlier, Calvin and Cath both have diagnoses of schizophrenia. Many people with similar experiences are given this or similar diagnoses by their doctors. According to conventional medical opinion, schizophrenia is one of the most common psychotic disorders, with approximately 1% of the population suffering from this disorder at some point in their lives. This means that, in the United Kingdom alone, about 600,000 people will have a diagnosis of schizophrenia (the figure for the USA is just under 3 million). Similar rates apply to other psychotic disorders – bipolar disorder (or manic depression) affects up to 2% of the population (so over 1 million people in the UK or about 6 million in the USA) and schizoaffective disorder affects roughly 0.5% (about 300,000 people in the UK, about 1.5 million in the USA). With other psychotic disorders, such as psychotic depression and delusional disorder, this means that well over 2 million people in the UK will be affected by a psychotic condition that leads them to seek help from mental health services.

HOW COMMON IS IT TO HEAR VOICES?

Calvin was walking down the road last week and heard a voice saying 'He shouldn't be allowed out. Someone should get him'. When he looked around, there was nobody there. Yesterday, he was watching television and heard a voice telling him that the newsreader was talking about him. He changed channel to watch Top of the Pops, and the voice said 'They're singing about you now'.

The experience that Calvin has of hearing voices when nobody is around (or at least when nobody seems to be saying the words that he is hearing) is actually quite common. Sometimes the things said appear to come from neighbours, the television or radio, people passing in the street or even ghosts. At other times they might seem to come out of thin air. Voices may seem to come from behind, through the walls or even through loudspeakers. They often seem very real and can, at times, be very loud. They might shout or, on the other hand, they might whisper.

Voices can say all sorts of things. Sometimes what they say is not upsetting, and they can be very positive and supportive, but for some people they are anxiety-provoking, threatening or even abusive. If you hear voices that do not upset you, then there is no reason to consider them a problem. However, some people are disturbed by the experience of hearing voices. The voices may seem to talk about the hearer, even describing what he or she is doing or thinking. This type of experience can be very puzzling, as it may seem difficult to understand how the voices can know such personal things. They can be particularly distressing when they are rude or abusive. Sometimes they might swear or tell the hearer to do awful things.

There is some evidence that voices are a normal psychological phenomenon that can be experienced by almost anyone under the right circumstances. Hallucinations can be induced by drugs (such as cannabis, LSD and cocaine) or by alcohol withdrawal after a long period of heavy drinking. There are specific life stresses that appear to cause the experience of hallucinations (both seeing people and hearing voices), such as bereavement. One study, for example, found that over 80% of older people who had lost their partner had a visual or auditory hallucination (thought that they saw or heard their partner) in the month following the death [3].

Surveys suggest that 10–25% of the general population have had a hallucinatory experience at least once. A recent study of over 1,000 people with no psychiatric history found that 16% of these had heard voices – this figure implies that about 10 million people in Britain and about 47 million people in the USA have heard voices. A very large interview study of 17,000 adults in the USA [4] found that 4–5% of the general population experience hallucinations during any one year period – this figure implies that about 3 million people in Britain (and nearly 15 million in the USA) hear voices every year.

Studies assessing the occurrence of voices in college students have found that a large minority (37–39%) report such phenomena, and that these experiences are not related to mental health problems. One investigation found that 71% of the 375 students surveyed reported some experience of brief verbal hallucinations while awake [5].

Additional support for these findings comes from the work of a Dutch social psychiatrist, Marius Romme. He found that of the 173 people experiencing auditory hallucinations who had responded to a request on television, 39% were not in psychiatric care [6]. When considered together, these findings suggest that hearing voices is a much more common experience than doctors usually suppose and does not necessarily lead to a need for psychiatric care.

WHERE DO VOICES COME FROM?

Calvin started to hear voices when he was 18 years old. Just beforehand he had begun to recall an incident of sexual abuse from his childhood. He found these memories very distressing and he had trouble sleeping. In order to try to help himself sleep, and in the hope of feeling calmer during the daytime, he started to smoke a lot of cannabis. When the voices started, he found that they said supportive things to him, such as 'You'll be okay' and 'It wasn't your fault'. He thought that the voices might be supernatural friends, who were trying to protect him.

A number of factors seem to be associated with the onset of hearing voices [7], and some of these were present in Calvin's case. These include:

- The recent experience of bereavement
- Experience of sexual abuse during childhood or adulthood
- Experience of other kinds of severe trauma (such as physical assault, combat or kidnap)
- Solitary confinement
- Sleep deprivation
- The use of certain drugs (such as speed, cocaine, cannabis or LSD)
- A very high temperature or other physical illness
- Being on the verge of getting to sleep or waking up

Marius Romme reported that the majority of patients that he saw developed their voices following a traumatic event, and he suggests that hearing voices may be part of a coping process. This certainly would be one way of viewing the development of Calvin's voices.

Although it can be very difficult to believe at times, voices that nobody else can hear are sometimes misinterpretations of other sounds. They may also involve a misinterpretation of one's own thoughts, so that they sound as if someone is speaking aloud. This does not necessarily mean that the voices sound like one's own voice. They may be memories of someone else's voice. It may be a man's voice, a woman's voice or even a child's voice. The easiest way to understand this is to think about dreaming. In our dreams we can hear other people speaking. There are also other examples of sounds that we can vividly recall or experience; these include memories of other people speaking, when we deliberately imagine a conversation with someone we know well, or when we are unable to get a tune from the radio out of our minds. These examples show that we may, under certain circumstances, be able to experience our own thoughts as if they were the voice of someone else. It appears that this is most likely to happen under certain circumstances, such as following sleep problems, being stressed or taking drugs.

There are many research findings that support this account. For example, brain scans have shown that, when people are hearing voices, there is activity in the brain regions that normally control speaking [8]. Other studies have shown that the speech muscles move when people hear voices, in much the same way that they move when we talk to ourselves or think in words (this phenomenon is called *subvocalization*, and is similar to what happens when we read or pray silently). Finally, some research studies suggest that, if people deliberately engage in subvocalization (by counting to themselves, reciting poetry, doing crosswords etc.), then this disrupts the voices, often preventing them altogether. It therefore seems that voices are often 'inner speech' (or our own thoughts) that we experience as coming from someone or something else.

WHY DO SOME PEOPLE BECOME UPSET BY THEIR VOICES?

Calvin only began to be upset by his voices when he was admitted to hospital and was forced to take medication against his wishes. At this point, the voices changed from being supportive to being abusive and critical, saying things like 'He's mad', 'He'll never get out of hospital' and

'Someone should give him a good kicking'. He started to worry that the voices were actually neighbours of his or other patients on the ward who intended to harm him because of his racial origins.

Although many people hear voices and are not disturbed by them in any way, and may actually value the experience, some people become extremely upset by them. This may be the result of a change in life circumstances or an increase in stress. This could have been the case for Calvin, since being admitted to a psychiatric hospital can be a very frightening experience. If people believe that their voices are coming from someone powerful or someone who means them harm, then this can understandably be very disturbing (in Calvin's case, it is not surprising that he became upset when he believed that his neighbours wanted to cause him harm).

Some people get upset by the actual content of what their voices say (Calvin's voices were clearly threatening), whereas other people become upset because the voices are very distracting and prevent them from being able to do things like concentrate, have a conversation or get to sleep. The reason that experiences like hearing voices can be upsetting will be explored in more detail in later chapters.

HOW COMMON IS IT TO FEEL PARANOID?

We have seen that Cath is a 41-year-old woman with two grown-up children, and has been in contact with psychiatric services for 22 years since the birth of her first child. At this time she believed that social services were spying on her in order to gain information and take her son into care. She coped with this episode but suffered a recurrence of these beliefs two years later following the birth of her daughter, Claire. Cath's difficulties have continued over the years and she now believes that the police are working with social services to plan her prosecution. She believes that they let themselves into her house if she goes out and rearrange items to remind her that they are watching her. As a result she rarely leaves her house.

Ideas or beliefs that a doctor would call 'delusions' are also a very common symptom of schizophrenia; the most common type are delusions of persecution or paranoid beliefs – these occur when people believe that someone is deliberately trying to harm them. Over 60% of people with a diagnosis of schizophrenia have such beliefs.

These kinds of beliefs are also remarkably common in the general population [9]. For example, research has shown that about 25% of people with no history of using mental health services have thoughts about someone persecuting them (this would mean about 15 million people in the UK and about 74 million in the USA) and about 10% have thoughts that there is a conspiracy against them (about 6 million people in the UK and 30 million people in the USA). Of course, most people have milder feelings of being unfairly disliked from time to time – for example, when entering a room full of strangers.

HOW COMMON IS IT TO HAVE OTHER KINDS OF UNUSUAL BELIEFS?

Calvin sometimes worries that people on the television or radio are talking about him.

There are many other sorts of unusual beliefs. The most common of these in people with a diagnosis of schizophrenia are delusions of reference, in which people worry that other people, the television or radio, magazines or newspapers are talking about them (found in about 70% of patients). Delusions of control, where people believe that their actions are being controlled by someone or something else (such as God, the Devil, aliens or other people) are also common, being found in about 50% of patients. Other common unusual beliefs include thinking that one's thoughts are being broadcast, thinking that thoughts are being put in one's head and thinking that one has been chosen for a task, or is very special in some way.

In a survey of 60,000 British adults, it was found that beliefs in unscientific or parapsychological phenomena were commonly held [10]. For example, 50% of the sample expressed a belief in thought transference between two people (telepathy) and 25% believed in ghosts. Other studies have shown that between 30 and 80% of people agree to some extent with some ideas that doctors often describe as delusional. For example, in one study [11] it was found that 42% of people believe that others are dropping hints about them (about 25 million in the UK and 124 million in the USA), 46% believe in telepathy (about 28 million in the UK and about 136 million in the USA) and 5% believe that the TV or magazines have special messages directed at them personally (about 3 million people in the UK and about 15 million in the USA).

WHERE DO DELUSIONAL BELIEFS COME FROM?

It is likely that stress plays a part in the development of unusual beliefs. A person's culture and general belief system is also likely to play a part; for example, it is unlikely that someone who has not had a religious upbringing would worry about being controlled by the Devil, and someone who had never believed in extra-terrestrial life would be unlikely to worry about aliens beaming thoughts into their head.

Psychologists have shown that, contrary to popular belief, delusions are not held with absolute certainty and vary in terms of how upsetting they are, how much of the time people think about them and how much effort they may make to resist these thoughts [12]. It has also been shown that patients experiencing delusional beliefs tend to jump to conclusions, and have a rapid, overconfident reasoning style [13]; in other words, people with unusual beliefs make decisions about the causes of events very quickly and tend to stick to the first explanation for an event that springs to mind. It has been found that paranoid beliefs, in particular, tend to occur when people blame other people for negative life experiences [14], and it is thought that this style of reasoning may help to protect against low self-esteem (if you blame somebody else when something goes wrong you do not have to blame yourself).

In Cath's case, it is possible that her worries about her children may have led her to feeling that she deserved to be punished in some way. It may be that by blaming the police and social services for bad things that happen now, she in some way avoids blaming herself (and, therefore, protects her self-esteem). It may also be the case that she made sense of a coincidence, such as getting a letter from social services when there was a helicopter overhead, by assuming that there was a conspiracy involving the police and social services because that was the first idea that popped into her mind. While other people may have dismissed this as just an unrealistic thought, it could be that her style of thinking made her stick with this explanation.

WHY DO SOME PEOPLE BECOME UPSET BY THEIR UNUSUAL BELIEFS?

In one study of unusual ideas [15], it was found that it was not the content of beliefs that distinguished patients on a psychiatric ward from members of the general public, but rather the degree of certainty (how much they thought that their belief was true), distress and preoccupation (the extent to which they could not stop thinking about it). This suggests that it is how such thoughts are interpreted that makes the difference between psychotic patients and the general population rather than the thoughts themselves. In other words, the more attention people pay to unusual thoughts, the more certain they are that their thoughts must be true, and the more significance they attribute to them, the more likely they are to become distressed and seek psychiatric help.

In Cath's case, she believed that the social services and the police were trying to persecute her with about 90% certainty, and she thought about these ideas a lot of the time – as a result, she was frequently upset. If she could view these ideas as unlikely to be accurate, and was able to dismiss them from her mind, it is likely that she would not be nearly so distressed. In later chapters, we will examine how she might be able to develop skills to help her achieve this.

ARE MY OWN EXPERIENCES ABNORMAL?

In this and later chapters of this book, we will ask you to carry out some exercises that may help you with any psychotic problems you have been experiencing.

Do you have any similar experiences to the ones described in this chapter? If so, what are they?

_____
_____
_____
_____

How common do you think they are? Base your decision on the information presented in this chapter.

Your experiences or beliefs	Percentage of population that have similar experiences	How many people would have this experience in the United Kingdom (population is about 60 million people in total)

When you first started to have these experiences, were there any factors (perhaps that other people noticed) that were associated with their onset (tick any that apply)?

- [ ] Bereavement
- [ ] Sexual abuse during childhood
- [ ] Sexual abuse during adulthood
- [ ] Physical assault during childhood
- [ ] Physical assault during adulthood
- [ ] Severe emotional abuse or bullying
- [ ] Combat or kidnap
- [ ] Solitary confinement or social isolation
- [ ] Sleep deprivation
- [ ] Using drugs (such as speed, cocaine, cannabis, ecstasy)
- [ ] Using hallucinogenic drugs (such as magic mushrooms or LSD)
- [ ] A very high temperature or other physical illnesses

SHOULD I SEEK HELP?

If unusual experiences are as common as the evidence discussed earlier seems to suggest, it follows that many people with these kinds of experiences get by perfectly well without seeking help. In deciding whether you want to seek help for your experiences, the following questions are likely to be helpful.

1. How am I feeling? If the experiences are making you feel anxious, angry, sad or distressed, then it may be worth thinking about what has been happening to you, and considering whether you want to seek some help for your problems. Alternatively, you may decide to take steps to resolve your difficulties on your own.
2. Am I able to do the things that I want to do? If there are things that you would like to be doing, such as seeing friends, going out, going shopping or getting a job, and if your worries about your experiences are preventing you from doing them – then it is worth considering whether or not to take some kind of action.
3. Are my close relationships being affected? If your unusual experiences and distress are causing problems in your relationships with people that you care about, then tackling the experiences may have a positive effect on your relationships.
4. Is my sleep being affected? When you try to sleep at night, are you finding certain worries going round and round in your mind, causing you to feel restless and unable to settle? Are you waking early and finding yourself unable to go back to sleep because of worries on your mind?

5. Am I feeling physically different than usual or how I would like to feel? Are you feeling more tired than usual? Are you experiencing palpitations, headaches, nausea, 'butterflies' in your stomach, feeling unable to concentrate, shaky etc. but can't think of any physical cause? These types of experiences may indicate you have worries on your mind, even if you are not aware of them.
6. Have others started to point out that I am acting differently than usual? If others whom you trust begin to point out that your behaviour, reactions or mood appear different from usual, it may be worth checking out whether there is anything on your mind that would explain this.

3

Will I be like this forever?

At times, Cath looks back on her life and feels as if she has been suffering from her difficulties forever. After 22 years of feeling almost constantly frightened, it is difficult for her to recall the time before the birth of Steven and Claire, when she could enjoy the ordinary things in life, such as seeing friends and visiting the pub with her husband. Looking to her future, she can see very little to look forwards to, just year after year depending for protection and safety on a man whom she has long ago stopped loving, and who no longer appears to love her. Her pessimism about her future is linked to her beliefs about what has happened to her. After all, she thinks, if her tormentors have been after her for over 20 years, they are unlikely to ever stop.

Calvin, too, feels pessimistic about the future, although for very different reasons. Although he has only been receiving psychiatric care for about four years, like Cath he finds it difficult to remember the time before he was ill. Unlike Cath, he has gradually begun to accept the explanation of his difficulties offered by his doctors and nurses, who have persistently tried to persuade him that he suffers from an illness of the brain.

The problem for Calvin is that the doctors and nurses appear to be very pessimistic about his illness. Indeed, his consultant psychiatrist once told him (in a kindly voice – he obviously thought that it was better if Calvin did not have any unrealistic expectations) that he should accept that schizophrenia is a life-long condition, that no one ever completely recovers from it, and that he should accept his limitations and expect to take his medication for the rest of his days. This would not be so bad if the medication only had positive effects. However, as we saw in an earlier chapter, Calvin usually felt unmotivated and lacking in emotion when he took his medication.

The idea that psychosis is a life-long condition dates back to the earliest days of psychiatry, and continues to be accepted by many mental health professionals today. Indeed, Emil Kraepelin, the nineteenth-century psychiatrist who first introduced the concept of schizophrenia, believed that the condition is degenerative; in other words, that patients nearly always became more ill over time [16].

One reason why some mental health professionals continue to hold this pessimistic view is that they have been taught to think this way during their training. Another reason is that they tend to recall those patients whose difficulties have been most persistent, and who have therefore required continuing treatment. Patients who have short episodes and disappear from view, requiring no extra help, can be quickly forgotten. In order to understand what is really likely to happen to someone suffering from psychotic symptoms, it is best to look at some research.

In fact, very few studies have examined what happens to people with psychosis over very long periods of time; mainly because such studies are enormously difficult to carry out. However, those that have been carried out have all led to the same general conclusions:

1. *Outcome* (how well people do over time) turns out to be very difficult to define. This is because people do well or badly in different ways. For example, some people find that their symptoms go away over time, whereas others do not (symptom outcome); some people find that they are able to cope with a job, whereas others cannot (occupational outcome); and some people find that they can maintain rich networks of friends, whereas others become progressively more socially isolated (social outcome). Importantly, *these different kinds of outcomes do not seem to be very closely related to each other*. So, for example, one person may completely recover from her symptoms but feel unable to go to work, whereas another may feel able to follow a rich social life and maintain a career but may still, for example, suffer from hearing voices.
2. *Outcome is enormously variable*, no matter what the diagnosis. So, for example, some people completely recover from their symptoms, whereas others continue to be affected over long periods of time. As a rough rule of thumb, about one-third of patients in Europe and North America seem to completely recover, whereas about one in four remain ill. The remaining patients (just over a third) have intermediate outcomes, either experiencing mild symptoms over long periods of time or being well for much of the time but occasionally experiencing episodes of severe symptoms. As many of the people in this last group can cope well with the demands of ordinary life, it is reasonable to say that more than half of those who seek psychiatric help for psychosis feel reasonably happy for long periods of their lives.
3. *Complete recovery can occur many, many years after the onset of difficulties*. A recent World Health Organization study, which examined patients 15 years and 25 years after they first became ill, found that many of those patients who remained ill after 15 years had recovered by the end of 25 years.
4. Surprisingly, when patients living in non-industrialized countries (for example, Nigeria or rural China) have been compared with patients living in industrialized countries (for example, Britain or the USA), it has generally been found that *more patients recover in the non-industrialized nations*. The explanation for this has been hotly debated, but many psychologists and psychiatrists believe it is because patients living in non-industrialized countries experience less stress, are less discriminated against (and so are more able to return to their lives afterwards) or because society and families are more supportive.

Eventually, Calvin was fortunate to find a new psychiatrist, Dr Skinner, who seemed to know about the latest research, and who took the time to explain it in language that Calvin could understand. This discussion was actually triggered by Calvin himself, who realized that meeting his new doctor for the first time provided an ideal opportunity to ask some questions that had been worrying him for some time. Before he went into the meeting, he was very nervous and even worried that the doctor might tell him off for asking questions. However, he was so determined to get some answers that he wrote his questions down on a piece of paper to make sure that he did not forget them.

As things turned out, the doctor could not have been nicer. On noticing how anxious Calvin was, the doctor immediately tried to put him at his ease. He told Calvin that he would try to answer as many of his questions as possible in the quarter of an hour available, but would offer him a special appointment if he needed more time. Just the fact that the doctor was taking so much trouble made Calvin feel valued.

When Calvin said that he was frightened about what might happen to him in the future, the doctor smiled knowingly, and then explained about the long-term studies carried out. He told Calvin that he should be optimistic about the future, and pointed out that, so far, he had managed to cope with some very frightening experiences very well. Calvin agreed to meet the doctor on a second occasion, as suggested, when they would try to work out how to maximize Calvin's chance of complete recovery.

As Calvin walked away from the meeting, he felt better than at any time since he first became ill. He felt empowered to influence his own future, and optimistic about what was likely to happen to him in the years to come.

4

What's happening to me?

Cath received a letter from the Department of Social Security (DSS) about the disability allowance she had been receiving. It asked her to attend an appointment to ensure her payments continued and gave her an appointment time. She felt very anxious as she set out for this appointment.

On walking down the road Cath began to worry that the police helicopters that she heard overhead were trying to read her mind to gain information about her personal relationships. She was concerned that they would try to use any information against her should she ever be taken to court. As a result, she became very anxious and began to experience palpitations. She became more anxious on feeling these physical sensations, as she believed they may have been the result of the radio waves being 'beamed down' from the helicopter.

Cath looked at the pavement and counted the slabs, as she believed that this would block the surveillance from the helicopter. Whilst walking, Cath arrived at the main road at the same time as a police car drove past, and was so convinced that this was part of the same scheme that she turned about and returned home, looking at the pavement and counting all the way. She failed to respond to the next three letters from the DSS because of what had happened on this occasion.

As a result of failing to attend appointments or respond to the DSS, Cath received a letter stating that some of her benefits would be stopped. Cath believed that the reduction in her benefits was a result of the conspiracy between the police and social services, who wanted to punish her for crimes in her youth.

Incidents of the sort described above occur fairly commonly in the lives of people with psychosis. If you have been suffering from the kind of difficulties we have described in the last three chapters, it is possible that you have had experiences similar to Cath's. Perhaps you have found yourself terrified by some particular combination of events, which has led you to feel that you are under some kind of threat. Perhaps, like Cath, as a consequence of this experience, you have felt forced to follow a course of action that proved to only make your problems worse. In this chapter, we will explore how these kinds of incidents happen. So let's begin by considering what was happening to Cath, in the way that a psychological therapist would do:

What really happened to Cath?

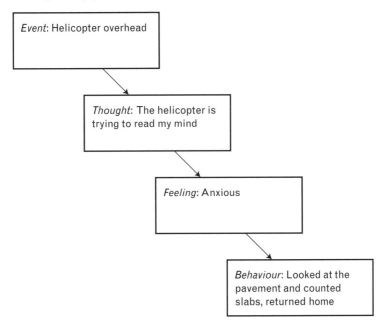

The diagram above tries to show what happened. The incident started when Cath set out for her appointment with the DSS. She was already anxious about the appointment. Once anxious, Cath was scanning her environment looking out for things that might be dangerous. When she heard the helicopter, she interpreted this to mean that the police and social services were spying on her. She was worried that they might be able to read her mind so, in order to prevent this happening, she looked at the pavement and counted the paving slabs. This unfortunately meant that Cath could no longer see what was happening around her, and was therefore unable to notice anything that was inconsistent with her fears (for example, that the helicopter was in fact hovering over the town centre, some distance away). As a result of her worries, Cath's anxiety increased and, as a consequence of this, she began to experience palpitations. Cath did not realize her palpitations were the result of anxiety and took them to be caused by the surveillance equipment that she believed was being carried by the helicopter. Thus, her palpitations seemed to further confirm her fears and increased her anxiety, so she returned home, never discovering whether bad things would have happened had she kept her appointment. Following this incident, Cath had her benefits reduced. Cath took this development to be further evidence for her beliefs about a police and social services conspiracy.

BREAKING DOWN PROBLEMS IN ORDER TO UNDERSTAND THEM: THE COGNITIVE THERAPY WAY

All of our difficulties have a number of factors. When something happens that triggers a negative feeling, the following sequence is usually elicited.

1. *An Event* happens and we seek to understand it.
2. *Thoughts*. These are the thoughts that go through your mind following the event, for example, we think about what the recent event says about us, what others are thinking or what we imagine the consequences of events may be.
3. *Feelings*. This concerns how we feel in ourselves – whether we feel sad, worried, angry or frightened.
4. *Behaviours*. This concerns what we do as a result of how we feel, something that happens or a thought that we have. It can be something that we do physically, like keeping our head down and not looking at people, or something we do inside our head, like singing to ourselves or trying not to think about something upsetting.

In turn, our reactions to events will also affect our environment, as in Cath's example – she did not go to the DSS and then her benefits were stopped. These changes in our environment can bring about further changes in the way we think about the world.

These factors are all linked and affect each other. By understanding these links and the way that the factors are related, we can begin to work out how small changes in one factor can have a knock-on effect on other areas of our experience. All being well, we should be able to improve all areas of our difficulties by concentrating our efforts on one or two factors. This is what cognitive therapy usually involves.

Cognitive therapy, which was first developed by Dr Aaron T. Beck in the USA, involves examining the links between events, thoughts, feelings and behaviour in order to see whether these relationships can be changed in some way to help reduce distress and improve quality of life. Research has shown that how we understand (think) or make sense of our problems has an effect on how we feel (emotion), act and cope with them (behaviour) [17]. This model can be applied to the kind of problems we considered in the previous chapters [18], and cognitive therapy based on this model has been successfully used to help people with distressing psychotic experiences such as hearing voices and unusual beliefs [19]. Suppose that, at some difficult time in your life, you began to have unusual experience (for example, voices) that you had not previously experienced. If, as a consequence, you believed that others were trying to harm you, you may have felt frightened, and suffered from feelings of tension and other anxiety symptoms such as palpitations. You may even have stopped leaving your home in an attempt to remain safe.

Alternatively, if you saw the voices as a normal experience, perhaps indicating that you had been under considerable stress, you would probably have experienced much less anxiety. As a consequence, you may have experienced less tension and may have been more able to continue doing all the things you normally enjoy doing.

The general principle is that the way that we think about events or an experience affects the way that we feel (our mood) and what we do (our behaviour). These in turn affect our environment so, for example, if we stop going out, we can lose contact with friends and have fewer people around to help us cope with our difficulties.

In turn, these areas of our functioning continue to affect each other. For example, once our mood is low, this affects the way we think. On a day on which we feel very low we might walk down the road and walk past a friend on the other side. If we waved to this friend and the friend failed to wave back, we might then see this as a sign that they did not like us. Alternatively, on a good day we might think that the friend was probably preoccupied or distracted, did not have her glasses on or was upset about something. However, thinking our friends do not like us, instead of thinking of a more neutral interpretation of the encounter, will almost certainly make us feel more miserable.

In general, once our mood is lowered, it affects the way we process information in three main ways. Firstly, we tend to notice all the negative things that happen around us rather than the positive things, and we can also find ourselves looking out for anything bad around us. Secondly, our memory is affected so that we tend to remember all the bad things that have happened to us, forgetting the good things. Finally, we tend to interpret our experiences in the most negative way possible.

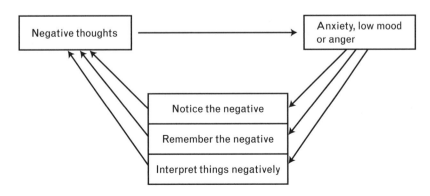

A vicious circle can therefore easily be created, whereby negative or anxious thoughts can lead us to become sadder or more fearful and as a result of this, the way we see the world is affected. In the same way this changes mood and so the cycle continues.

CALVIN'S EXPERIENCES

Calvin received a letter one morning from his community mental health team informing him that his key worker, Philip, would be away until further notice and that another nurse would be coming to meet with him the following week. Calvin was unsettled by this development but accepted it. Later that night, Calvin's voices became abusive and told him that his key worker had left or become ill because of something that Calvin had done. Over the next few days, Calvin's voices became more and more critical and he became very concerned that something had happened to Philip and that he was in some way responsible. He began to feel very anxious and guilty and, as a result, stopped going to the drop-in centre or attending his normal daily activities. Instead, he spent time trying to work out what he had done wrong. Eventually, his sleep became affected and he began to stay awake through the night, going over past events in his mind in order to understand what had happened. By the time the nurse arrived, Calvin was convinced that something terrible was happening for which he was to be blamed.

When Amanda, his new nurse, arrived, she was able to explain to him that his previous key worker Philip had taken long-term leave due to a series of bereavements in his family that had required him to become a carer for young children at home. She explained to Calvin that this had nothing to do with him. Together they sat down and tried to understand why Calvin was becoming increasingly distressed throughout the week.

So let's see what was happening for Calvin:

So let us look again at a diagram describing these events. Once Calvin began thinking that he was in some way responsible for Philip leaving, he began to feel anxious and guilty. As a result of this, he began to try to think of everything he had ever said to Philip. However, because Calvin was so anxious, he was only able to remember all the times they had disagreed or when Calvin had been upset about something (this type of selective *memory bias* is common in people suffering from emotional difficulties). Additionally, whatever he did remember, he interpreted as evidence that he had upset Philip (this is an *interpretation bias*). Both of these biases led him to become more and more convinced that it was his fault that Philip had left and indeed, that he had done something terrible

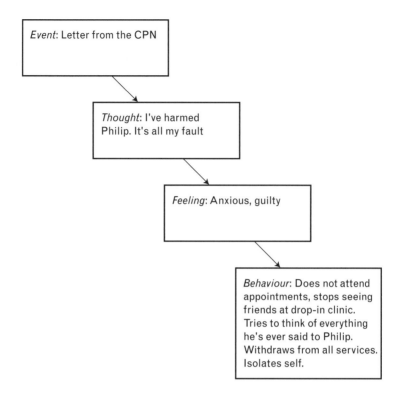

to harm or upset him. Calvin was so upset and brooded on this so much that his sleep became affected, and he became very tired. As a consequence, his voices became more frequent and Calvin was much less able to think clearly and began to blame himself further. Calvin then began to withdraw from all services and did not reply to any letters from the new nurse. This prevented Calvin from finding out the reasons why Phillip had had to leave and that it had had absolutely nothing to do with him.

Feelings

In general, strong emotions have an important purpose – they alert us to the need to deal with challenges that we encounter in life. For example, the feeling of fear may prepare us for facing an imminent threat, and the feeling of excitement may make us alert in preparation for some kind of adventure. This principle applies equally in ordinary life and when we experience the kinds of difficulties that lead us to seek psychiatric help.

Before proceeding, it is worth noting that some psychiatrists and psychologists have held that it is the *absence* of feelings that is problematic in some types of psychosis. In conventional psychiatric textbooks, it is sometimes said that manic depression/bipolar disorder can be distinguished from schizophrenia because in the former condition emotions are excessive, whereas in the latter they are absent. Indeed, most psychiatric textbooks list *flat affect* as a symptom of schizophrenia.

In fact, this idea is almost completely false. Certainly, some people seem to look as though they are lacking feelings, but research has shown that this is almost always a problem of *emotional expression*. The emotions of patients with flat affect are as strong as – often stronger than – those of people without mental health problems. These research findings are consistent with our clinical experience. When we see patients for psychological treatment they are often extremely unhappy. Indeed, it is often patients' interpretations of their unusual experiences – and the distress they experience as a consequence – that drives them to seek treatment.

HOW AM I FEELING?

Strangely, it might sometimes be difficult to work out how you are feeling, especially if you have been experiencing problems for a long time. This is because, when stressed and troubled, it can be difficult to focus on your inner world, or to think about your own emotions. Problem feelings can usually be described with just one word. Examples are listed below (there are others that may be more relevant to how you feel):

Sad	Panicky	Upset
Worried	Fearful	Embarrassed
Anxious	Miserable	Furious
Angry	Depressed	Irritated
Scared	Guilty	Suspicious
Ashamed	Terrified	Apprehensive

It is helpful to decide which feeling you are experiencing, as this may help you to work out how it is connected to the other aspects of your difficulties, for example underlying patterns of thinking (we will explain how you can do this later in the book). It is useful to start by noticing when your mood changes or when unpleasant feelings get worse; it can also be useful to start noticing different levels of negative moods. One way of doing this is by keeping a diary in which you rate your moods on a 0–100 scale, with 0 indicating that you have no negative emotion and 100 being the most anxious/depressed/angry that you have ever been. For example, when rating anxiety, scores might be recorded as follows:

0	10	20	30	40	50	60	70	80	90	100
No anxiety at all		A little anxiety		Quite a lot of anxiety			Very high anxiety			The most anxiety ever experienced

All of us at times feel a range of negative moods and emotions. This scale can help you to decide whether your emotional state is problematic for you or if it is more or less severe than anxiety you have felt in similar situations in the past.

It is possible that you notice yourself becoming tense in a particular situation. You may begin to hunch your shoulders, feel sweaty and tingly, or begin to feel your hands start to fidget and be unable to sit still and concentrate. At times like this it may be useful to take stock of the situation. Look around you and ask yourself questions such as:

> *When did this begin and what was I doing at the time?*
> *Who was I with and where was I?*
> *What feeling was I experiencing and how strong was this feeling?* (For this it may be useful to go back to our list of feelings and to rate those most relevant on our 0–100 scale.)

One day, Cath received a letter from her GP inviting her to have a routine check-up with her family doctor. As the day for this appointment drew nearer, she began to experience difficulties sleeping, nausea and a churning sensation in her stomach. Her CPN came round and together they began to fill in the following table, which Cath had been given by her therapist.

Event: (What am I doing? Who am I with?)
Got an appointment to go to have a GP check-up
Feeling: (What emotion am I experiencing?)
Fear
How strong is this feeling?
0   10   20   30   40   50   60   70   80   90   100

You can find your own version of this form in the Appendix.

SO WHAT IS THE ROLE OF THINKING?

Following receipt of this letter from her GP inviting Cath for a routine check-up, Cath had begun to get more and more anxious. She eventually contacted her CPN and together they decided that it was important to try to work out what was causing her increasing distress.

Her CPN accompanied her to her local community mental health centre and there they met with Cath's therapist. The therapist asked to look at the record that Cath had filled in with her CPN.

Event: (What am I doing? Who am I with?)

Got an appointment to go to have a GP check-up

Feeling: (What emotion am I experiencing?)

Fear

How strong is this feeling?

								X		
0	10	20	30	40	50	60	70	80	90	100

On looking at the table it became apparent that she was experiencing fear at 75 out of 100. This is a very strong emotion and one that most people would not experience on receiving a letter from a GP about a check-up. Therefore, Cath and her therapist decided it would be useful to understand why this letter had caused so much anxiety.

Therapist: Shall we talk about what was happening for you when you received that letter?

Cath: Yes, but I have no idea why I feel so bad.

Therapist: So where were you when you received the letter and what were you doing?

Cath: Well, it was a Monday morning and I was at home cleaning out the bathroom. I heard the postman and went down to see what had arrived.

Therapist: So you got the letter and opened it. What was your first reaction?

Cath: Shock, my heart started beating and I felt really wobbly. I had to go and sit down.

Therapist: I'd like you to imagine yourself back there, seeing this letter for the first time. What is going through your mind when you look at it?

Cath: I'm wondering why they have sent me this letter now.

Therapist: And if you had to answer that question, why do you think they sent the letter at that time?

Cath: I'm not sure, but there must be more to it than just a routine check-up.

Therapist: So you're thinking it's not just a routine check-up?

Cath: Yeah, no one else gets these letters, I bet it's not even from the GP and if it is, someone must have put them up to it.

Therapist: And have you got any ideas who that might be?

Cath: Well, it's probably the police; this might be their way of checking up on me. You know, to get more information on what I've been up to.

Therapist: And if the police were doing this to check up on you, what might happen?

Cath: They'll know for certain about things I've done in the past, they have a case against me and I'll be arrested. . . . I just can't bear it, prison. . . . I just couldn't cope with that . . .

Therapist: That sounds like a really scary thought for you, no wonder you've been feeling so frightened. If I had those thoughts, I'd be really frightened too. I wonder if I could ask you how much you believe each of the thoughts.

The therapist now took each of the thoughts in turn and asked about how much Cath believed in each of them:

Thought	Belief in thought
The police are behind this letter	90%
They are doing it to make a case against me	90%
I'll be arrested	70%
I'll be sent to prison	50%

THOUGHTS (OR HOW WE INTERPRET EVENTS)

Once we know Cath's thoughts, it's easy to see why receiving a routine letter from her doctor made her so anxious. Anyone interpreting the letter in a similar way would have been affected in the same way, especially if the thoughts expressed beliefs that are held with great certainty. In later chapters we will discover that, even when our beliefs are held with great certainty, they may not accurately describe the world. Under these circumstances, it may be possible to examine them and replace them with more realistic thoughts.

This type of making sense of events described by Cath is called automatic thinking [17, 20]. We all have automatic thoughts that arrive in the mind out of the blue and without any effort. Some automatic thoughts, however, can make us feel anxious, depressed or angry. It is because they arrive without warning that they can sometimes be very difficult to consider and examine. However, we will see that, once we understand how they are connected to strong negative emotions, we can do something about them.

Automatic thoughts can take the form of *words* (e.g. the thought that 'The police are out to get me' or 'I'll be sent to prison'); they can be *images* or pictures in the mind (e.g. in Cath's case an image of herself being bundled into a police car); or they can be in the form of *memories* (e.g. Cath may have remembered a remark made by a teacher years ago about law breakers being sent to prison).

SO HOW DO WE IDENTIFY AUTOMATIC THOUGHTS?

The best time to identify automatic thoughts is when there is a strong emotional change, for example if you suddenly notice a big increase in your levels of anxiety, a surge of anger, or a sudden drop in mood [17, 20]. At this time it can be useful to ask yourself the following questions:

What was going through my mind when I started to feel like this?
What do I imagine is the worst that might happen?
If this does happen, what is the worst thing about it?
What does this say about me and the future?
Am I worrying about what others will think or do?
What images or memories come to mind in this situation?

It can also be very useful to fill in a thought record [20, 21], such as those shown below.

Calvin was listening to the radio one day, when his voices began to comment that the radio announcer was talking about him. He began to listen very carefully to what was being said on the radio. The more he did this, the more he heard things that related to his life. The radio mentioned Birmingham, the city in which he had been born. There was an advert for the Ford Focus car, and his present house was next to a billboard with an advert for this car. The radio announcer mentioned football and, only recently, Calvin's CPN had just persuaded him to join a five-a-side group at his local drop-in centre. Hearing these things, Calvin became distressed and angry. The next day he discussed his feelings with his CPN, who suggested that they fill out a thought record.

Event	Thoughts	Feeling	Behaviour
What happened?	What was going through your mind? What are you worrying is the worst that might happen? What images or memories come to mind in this situation?	What were you feeling? How strong was it 0–100?	What did you do?
At home listening to the radio. The radio talked about things that were relevant to me. I was alone.	The radio announcer is talking about my life 70% He is using my life for material for his radio show 70% He is getting famous at my expense 60% They should pay me 90% They are exploiting me 85%	Fear 40 Anger 90	Shouted at radio announcer Turned radio off

Once they had completed the thought record, it became apparent to Calvin and his CPN why Calvin felt so upset and so angry. The record allowed them to make sense of his emotions. It is worth noting that some thoughts are often more obviously connected to emotions and behaviours than others. It is often useful to ask yourself which of the thoughts you record make best sense of your bad feelings. These will be the thoughts that we need to concentrate on.

BEHAVIOURS

Calvin's voices often say unpleasant, abusive and critical things to him. He frequently worries that the voices are his neighbours or people he has met through his contact with mental health services (other patients or staff). When the voices threaten him, saying things like 'Let's get him', 'He's going to go mad again and end up in hospital' and 'We'll wait until he's not expecting it and then we'll kill the weirdo', he understandably feels very frightened.

At times like this, Calvin understandably adopts certain ways of behaving in order to try to protect himself from the voices and from the things that he fears will happen. For example, he will usually go out wearing baggy clothes and a big hood in the hope that the people he worries about will not recognize him, and, therefore, he will not be attacked. If he sees people that he is concerned about, he will usually try to stare them out in order to discourage them from attacking him. Whenever he is out of his flat, he will be on 'red alert' for signs of danger and people who might be going to attack him, so he constantly scans his environment for dangerous-looking people. When he is at home he will always make sure that all of the doors and windows are locked, and he has extra bolts and chains on his front door. When the voices talk about him ending up in hospital again, Calvin feels very scared because of his negative experiences of hospital in the past, so he does things to prevent this from happening: for example, he may take extra medication, lie down and try to go to sleep or try to distract himself from what the voices are saying.

Because Calvin believes that the voices might harm him or drive him mad, the behaviours that he adopts in order to prevent these things from happening make perfect sense. However, precisely because Calvin is frightened by his voices, his behaviours in response to them have some unfortunate consequences. Can you guess what these consequences are? The following story might help:

The village and the vampires

There is a remote village in the depths of Transylvania where all of the villagers believe in vampires. Their belief in vampires is so strong that all of the villagers keep strings of garlic around their necks at all times, even when sleeping, in order to keep the vampires away. They all have a crucifix in every room of their house. They also spray themselves twice a day with holy water, and wash their clothes and sheets with water that has a drop of holy water in it. They do this because, as everyone knows, vampires are afraid of garlic, crucifixes and holy water. The villagers have always taken these precautions for as long as anyone can remember, and no one in the village has ever seen or been attacked by a vampire. Because no one has seen a vampire, they know that the things that they are doing in order to stay safe and keep the vampires away have been working. They would never choose to stop doing these things, fearing that to do so might allow the vampires into the village.

A number of questions might help you to think about whether the villagers' methods of protecting themselves against vampires create any difficulties for them:

> What do you make of the villagers' beliefs about vampires?
>
> What do you make of the villagers' beliefs about the garlic, crucifixes and holy water?
>
> How much time and effort do the villagers spend worrying about vampires and doing things to keep them away? How would they react if there was a shortage of garlic or holy water?
>
> What effect does using the garlic, crucifixes and holy water have on the villagers' belief about the vampires?
>
> How could the villagers find out whether vampires actually exist?

By now you should be able to see some parallels between the behaviour of the villagers in this story and the way that Calvin tries to protect himself from his voices. Is it possible that what Calvin does in order to prevent himself from being attacked is similar to the villagers' use of garlic, crucifixes and holy water? Also, is it possible that Calvin's behaviours actually prevent him from finding out that he will not be attacked, since he assumes that he has remained unhurt because he has carried out the protective actions?

When he goes out and is not attacked, Calvin thinks to himself, 'I wasn't attacked because they didn't recognize me' or 'If I hadn't stared at that man then he would have attacked me'. When the voices tell him he is going to go mad and end up in hospital, but this doesn't happen, he thinks to himself, 'I would have ended up in hospital if I hadn't had a lie-down and listened to my music' or 'If I hadn't taken that extra pill then I would have gone mad for sure'.

Calvin's efforts to protect himself may stop him from finding out that the things he fears will not happen. His behaviours, which are designed to make him feel safe (and which do make him feel safe in the short term), may actually make his worries about future attacks worse. Behaviours that make us feel safe in the short term, but which reinforce our belief in things that upset us in the long term, are called *safety behaviours* [22, 23].

What are Cath's safety behaviours?

You might remember that when she walks down the road, Cath sometimes worries that the police helicopters that she hears overhead are trying to read her mind in order to gain information about her personal relationships. She worries that they will try to use any information against her should she ever be taken to court. In order to prevent her thoughts being accessed by the helicopters, Cath looks at the pavement and counts the slabs, as she believes that this will block out the helicopter pilots' ability to read her mind.

What are Cath's safety behaviours? An obvious one is looking at the pavement and counting the slabs, which she hopes will prevent her mind from being read. What effect does this safety behaviour have on her belief that the helicopter pilots can read her mind? Although it makes her feel better in the short term, it prevents her from discovering that nothing bad will happen if she doesn't look down and count the slabs, with the consequence that she will continue to worry about helicopters whenever she goes out in the future.

What are my safety behaviours?

If you hear voices, the following questions might help you to identify your own safety behaviours.

My voices say the following kinds of things:

_____

_____

_____

_____

I believe that the voices are caused by or come from:

_____

_____

_____

_____

Hearing the voices means that:

_____

_____

_____

_____

What does hearing voices mean about me as a person?

_____

_____

_____

_____

Could anything bad happen to other people because of the voices?

_____
_____
_____
_____

Could anything bad happen to me because of the voices?

_____
_____
_____
_____

What is the worst thing that could happen because of the voices?

_____
_____
_____
_____

Do I do anything to stop these things from happening?

_____
_____
_____
_____

If you do not hear voices, but you have identified a worrying automatic thought in the previous section, the following questions might help you identify some safety behaviours.

What do you fear will happen? What is the worst thing that could happen?

_____
_____
_____
_____

Do you do anything to stop these things from happening?

_____
_____
_____
_____

Are there any similarities between some of the things that you do and the strategies used by the villagers in the story about The Village and the Vampires (above), or the safety behaviours used by Calvin and Cath?

_____

_____

_____

_____

The following questionnaire may also help you identify problematic safety behaviours. Below is a list of common safety behaviours people use when feeling threatened. Please read each statement and then circle the answer that applies to you. Please give a response to all the statements, and do not think about the answers for too long.

I avoid using public transport	yes	no
I avoid walking on the street alone	yes	no
I avoid enclosed spaces	yes	no
I avoid going to parties or out with friends	yes	no
I avoid going to the shops	yes	no
I drink alcohol if I feel threatened	yes	no
I try to relax or sleep if I feel threatened	yes	no
I listen to music if I feel threatened	yes	no
I try to ignore my thoughts about threat	yes	no
I pray to God when I feel threatened	yes	no
I think about religion when I feel threatened	yes	no
I make myself busy when I feel threatened	yes	no
I seek interaction with others when I feel threatened	yes	no
I isolate myself from others when I feel threatened	yes	no
I ask for help from the police	yes	no
I ask for help from friends or family	yes	no
I try to make people like me in order to feel safe	yes	no
I do whatever people say to avoid being threatened	yes	no
I threaten people who threaten me	yes	no
I do not always answer the door	yes	no
I check that all the doors in the house are locked	yes	no
I only go outside with others	yes	no
I keep my eyes to the ground when walking alone	yes	no
I walk quickly when alone	yes	no
When I go outside I wear certain things to make me feel safe	yes	no
When I go outside I watch what others are doing	yes	no
I escape situations if I don't feel safe	yes	no

CHAPTER 5

Evaluating your thoughts

As it is our interpretation of events that usually leads us to feel distress, rather than the events themselves, it makes sense to check out our interpretations to be certain that they are correct. We have already seen that once we are anxious, depressed or angry, the way that we process information can be affected. As a result of this it is possible that, especially when we are feeling emotional, our interpretations may not always be accurate. It is important to try to find out if this is the case as tackling an incorrect interpretation may lead to a significant reduction in distress. Cognitive therapy uses a number of common techniques to help us to evaluate the accuracy of our thoughts [19–21]; these techniques will be described along with exercises to help you to try them out.

CHECKING OUT WORRIES ABOUT THINGS THAT HAVE HAPPENED

As we saw in the last chapter, Cath became very anxious after receiving a letter from her GP inviting her for a routine health check-up. We discovered in the previous chapter that this was the result of her thinking that the police were behind this letter and were about to arrest her. This, of course, led Cath to become very anxious and frightened. As a result of this, Cath begun to notice anything that fitted with her concerns, such as TV programmes asking for witnesses in her local area (in reality due to a recent hit and run, which Cath had nothing to do with). She began to be preoccupied by memories of things she had done wrong in the past, and she began to interpret anything on TV or that anyone said to her as being an indication that there really was a conspiracy against her.

This cycle was explained to Cath by her therapist and she agreed that this might make her more likely to continue to believe in her fears. She agreed that it might be useful to look at the evidence supporting her worries and the evidence that might not be consistent with them.

The therapist gave Cath a sheet on which she could list all the evidence. Working together, they started by writing down Cath's troublesome automatic thought, recording how much she believed in it and also how anxious she was feeling. Cath then made a systematic list of the evidence. At the end of the sheet, there was a space for her to record her conviction in the thought and her anxiety, once the list had been completed.

Thought: The police sent the letter; they are doing it to make a case against me	**Belief conviction**: 90% **Anxiety**: 90%
Evidence supporting the thought	**Evidence NOT supporting the thought**
I was not expecting a letter	The letter said it was from my GP and was on NHS paper
I have never received a letter like this before	I've just turned 40 and haven't seen my GP for ages
I saw an appeal for witnesses on the TV yesterday	My neighbour said she got an invitation to a breast screening clinic out of the blue
I have done bad things in the past	In the past I've received invitations to immunizations and check-ups
	When the children were young I was always paranoid when the health visitor came to see them, but nothing bad ever happened
	The TV was asking for witnesses to a hit and run accident, and today the police announced that they had arrested someone for it
	Even though I've done bad things in the past, so far the police and lawyers have not been in touch with me
How much do you believe in the thought now? 40% *How anxious are you now?* 40% *Do you think this was a fact or just a thought?* A thought	

Cath was surprised to note that, just by completing the list, she had reduced both her certainty that the police were trying to make a case against her, and also her anxiety.

In this way Cath was able to evaluate the accuracy of her worries. This allowed her anxiety to reduce and enabled her to attend her appointment. Once she had attended this appointment, Cath was further reinforced that this was a routine health check-up and had nothing to do with previous events or the police.

At the end of the last chapter we asked you to try to identify one or more of your worrying thoughts. If you were successful, you can now make a list of the evidence supporting or not supporting the thought, just as Cath did with her therapist. A blank form for completing the list is provided below. When trying to generate evidence that does not fit with your anxious thought, it may be useful to ask yourself some of the following questions:

Is there anything that doesn't fit entirely with my original thought?

Is there anything that a friend, care co-ordinator or family member might suggest that doesn't fit with my thought?

Am I forgetting anything that proves that my original thought may not be true?

When I'm not in the particular situation that provoked the thought or am less anxious, do I think about this type of situation differently?

Have I had similar worrying thoughts about a threatening situation in the past, only to discover that nothing bad happened? What might this tell me?

Thought:	Belief conviction: Anxiety:
Evidence supporting the thought	**Evidence NOT supporting the thought**

How much do you believe in the thought now?
How anxious are you now?
Do you think this was a fact or just a thought?
Is there another possible explanation for this experience?

WORRIES ABOUT VOICES

Calvin left his house one morning to collect his benefits. He had been finding it increasingly difficult to leave the house due to his anxiety but had no food and no money and so needed to go to the post office. As he was walking down the road, he heard a voice shouting behind him saying 'Weirdo, you look really stupid'. Calvin turned around but could see no one. He thought that someone must be following him and out to get him, so he returned home without his money or any food. Calvin felt really anxious and upset, and was worried that without food he would become ill and be taken into hospital. He decided not to tell his support worker, as he believed that they would see this as him being unable to cope and again this would lead to a hospital admission.

When staff went in to see him, they found him unwell and hungry. They discussed his concerns regarding hospital and agreed that his current situation was not a cause for admission. Calvin agreed that his psychologist might visit him to help him overcome his fear of going out.

When the psychologist arrived a few days later, he helped Calvin complete a list of the evidence concerning whether he was being followed.

Thought: People are following me and trying to harm me	**Belief conviction**: 100% **Anxiety**: 96%
Evidence supporting the thought	**Evidence NOT supporting the thought**
The voices call me 'Weirdo' and tell me I look stupid	There was no one there behind me when I looked
The voices have threatened me before	I have heard voices before and no one has harmed me
	Other people I live with have heard voices and none of them have been harmed
	I hear voices when I'm in the house and I'm certain there's no one there
	In the past, I've decided that my voices are my own thoughts; also, I sometimes think I'm a weirdo

	I have had these voices for years and years and have always worried but nothing has happened and I have never been assaulted

How much do you believe in the thought now? 50%
How anxious are you now? 48%
Do you think this was a fact or just a thought? I think there are people following me, but it's not a fact.
Is there another possible explanation for this experience? It is possible that these voices are my own thoughts and worries and that if I were to leave the house nothing would happen.

Voices can be very confusing, as they may sound as if they come from outside your head, from objects around the house or even from space. Sometimes they sound like many different people. Other people hear a voice that sounds like their own voice or the voice of someone they know. Many people do not know that hearing our own thoughts and worries spoken out aloud can be quite normal. In these circumstances, it is not surprising that people hearing voices feel afraid and persecuted, perhaps concluding that other people are following them, or that they are being tormented by God or the Devil.

If you hear voices, you can use an evidence list to evaluate different possible explanations for your experiences, in much the same way that Cath evaluated the evidence for her belief that she was being persecuted by the police. On your own or with your therapist, first list all the possible explanations for your voices that come to mind, write out an evidence list for each explanation, and then decide which one best fits the facts.

Write down all possible explanations for the voices and rate (out of 100) how much you believe in each of these explanations.

Explanation for voices   Belief %

1. Own thoughts and worries

2.

3.

4.

Now complete the evidence list for each of the possible explanations.

Belief about voices:	Belief conviction: Anxiety:
Evidence supporting the belief	**Evidence NOT supporting the belief**
How much do you believe this now? *How anxious are you now?* *Is there another possible explanation for this experience?*	

Alternatively, you could do this for each possible explanation using this form:

Interpretation	Evidence for	Evidence against	Belief %	Associated feeling %

CHECKING OUT WORRIES ABOUT WHAT THE VOICES SAY

Even when we have reached an understanding about the source of the voices, it can still be difficult to deal with what they say. Often the content can be derogatory (saying bad things about yourself or about other loved ones) and therefore distressing. However, it is possible to learn to treat the content of the voices as thoughts rather than facts and in this section we will help you to do this. *Remember: What the voices say may not be true, just as our thoughts may be just thoughts and NOT facts.*

When the voices say things that upset you, take the following steps, using an evidence list:

What the voices say:	Belief conviction: Anxiety:
Evidence supporting the voices	Evidence **NOT** supporting the voices
How much do you believe this now? *How anxious are you now?* *Do you think this was a fact?* *Is there a more accurate statement that reflects the truth?*	

1. Write down what you are doing when you heard the voices and what the voices say.
2. On the evidence list, write down how much you believe what the voices say on a scale of 0–100, and also how anxious or upset this makes you on a scale of 0–100.
3. Now complete the evidence list, listing everything you can think of that is evidence in support of what the voices say, and also everything you can think of that is inconsistent with what the voices say.
4. Now, think about what the voices said. Can you be absolutely certain that this is 100% true? Is there any evidence that does not fit with what the voices say? Are there any facts that have been left out and that do not fit with what the voices say? Is there anything that a friend, family member or your therapist would point out that does not fit with what the voices said? Write this all down in the next column on the form.

5. Given what you have written on the evidence list, how true is what the voices said? If it's not true, what would be a more accurate statement to use that reflects the truth? Write this down.
6. Now, at the end of the evidence list, re-rate how much you believe in what the voices say and how upset or anxious you feel. In the final column rate your anxiety and upset on the same scale of 0–100 that you used before. Has your anxiety or upset decreased?

CHECKING OUT WORRIES ABOUT WHAT THE VOICES TELL YOU TO DO

Sometimes spoken thoughts or voices tell people what to do or what not to do. Some people's voices tell them to stay in the house, to say things to other people or tell them not to talk to their family or friends. Sometimes they urge people to hurt themselves or other people, or to do things that they are not happy to do. If you find yourself in this situation, it may seem frightening to disobey the voices, and you may be nervous about what will happen if you disobey the voices. However, we have already looked at the explanation for the voices and know that they might be internal thoughts experienced as if spoken out loud and made worse by current or past stress. Also, from looking at the content of voices, we might have found that what the voices say is very often not true.

If you experience voices and fear disobeying them, this problem can also be tackled with an evidence list. First, write down what you fear will happen.

Feared consequences of disobeying/not obeying voices

1.

2.

3.

Now use the evidence list to consider both the evidence that the feared consequence will happen and the evidence that it will not.

Constructing an evidence list can be a useful strategy whenever you have a worrying thought. In fact, you do not need to have any psychiatric problems to make use of it. It can be a good thing to do, for example, if you are worried about what someone else is thinking about you, or about something that is happening at work. Once you have completed your list, you can use it to reach a balanced view about what has been happening to you, as we will see in the next chapter.

EVALUATING EFFECTS ON FEELINGS

Once we have begun to get a feel for the evidence that both supports and does not support our worries, the next thing we can do is to see whether we can generate an alternative view that accounts for both types of evidence.

Once we become anxious, paranoid, angry or depressed, the way we process information changes. We begin to notice only negative information, remember only the bad things that have happened to us, and interpret anything that happens negatively. As a result, we are very likely to reach a mistaken conclusion about what is happening to us. Listing evidence, as we did in the last chapter, is the first step that we need to take to rectify this problem. Following on from this, our next step should be to form a more balanced view based on *all* of the evidence. It is important to note that we are not suggesting that it is good to indulge in mindless positive thinking, which can be as unrealistic as negative thinking. Rather that we need to cultivate *balanced* thinking that takes all of the available information into account.

As we have seen in recent chapters, Cath became very anxious after receiving a letter from her GP inviting her for a routine health check-up. She had taken this to mean that the police were after her and therefore began to notice, remember or interpret anything that happened as a sign that this was true. Therefore, in the last chapter, Cath decided to sit down with her therapist and look both at the evidence that fitted with her concerns and at the evidence that did not fit with her concerns. (Have a look at the evidence they generated earlier in the chapter.)

Cath and her therapist next tried to make sense of all the information that they had collected. They decided to write a summary of all the information in the 'evidence supporting thought' column and a summary of the information in the 'evidence NOT supporting thought' column. The following is what they came up with.

Evidence supporting the thought	Evidence **NOT** supporting the thought
I received an unexpected and unusual letter, which made me think about things I had done wrong in the past and other things happening at the moment.	The letter was on NHS paper and other people tell me they have received similar letters at similar times in their lives. I have also had similar worries when receiving letters in the past but these turned out to be genuine letters from health professionals. It appears that the TV ad was not at all related to me.

Cath's therapist then suggested that she try to combine the two statements to make one sentence that summed up all the evidence. Cath tried to form an *alternative* or *balanced view*:

Although the letter was unusual and unexpected and reminded me of things in the past, it was on NHS paper and other people have received similar letters. Other letters that I have worried about in the past have turned out to be genuine and been about what they said.

Once they had done this, Cath's therapist asked her to rate how much she believed her new balanced thought and also to re-rate her belief in her original thought. Finally, she asked Cath to re-rate her anxiety given this new balanced thought. The results of this exercise were:

Belief in the new balanced thought: 70%
Belief in the previous worrying thought: 15%
Anxiety now: 20%

REACHING YOUR OWN ALTERNATIVE OR BALANCED VIEW

Earlier in the book, we asked you to identify one or more worrying thoughts, and to list the evidence for and against them. You can now follow the steps taken by Cath and her therapist to reach a balanced view of the evidence relating to any of these thoughts. To do this, it will be helpful to proceed in the following steps (which we have adapted from Christine Padesky and Denis Greenberger's excellent book for people suffering from depression, *Mind Over Mood* [20]) using the evidence list you generated (the blank evidence list form in the Appendix provides you with a space to do this):

Summary of evidence supporting the automatic thought	Summary of evidence NOT supporting the automatic thought
The balanced view:	
Belief in the balanced thought: *Belief in the anxious thought:* *Anxiety now:*	

1. Write a summary of the evidence at the bottom of the column that supports your anxious thought.
2. Write a summary of the evidence at the bottom of the column that does NOT support your anxious thought.
3. Try to combine the two statements into one sentence, for example putting the word 'and' between the sentences, or by writing *Although (summary 1), the evidence suggests (summary 2)* . . .
4. Read this through a few times and re-write it until it sounds right to you and appears to sum up all the evidence you have gathered.
5. How much do you believe this new balanced thought? Rate this from 0 to 100%.
6. How much do you now believe your initial anxious thought? Rate this from 0 to 100%.
7. Now re-rate your levels of anxiety given all the new evidence you have found and your new balanced thought. Rate this from 0 to 100%.

At the end of this process, when you re-rate your mood, compare this with the previous level of anxiety you experienced. See whether this has changed. It may have changed, but there may be some degree of negative emotion still remaining, as was with the case for Cath. If this is the case, you might want to repeat the exercise looking for more information. You might also want to try a behavioural experiment, as described later in this book. Alternatively, it may be that there are some concerns that need to be tackled using an action plan, which will also be described later in the book.

CALVIN'S ALTERNATIVE BALANCED VIEW

Calvin had left his house one morning to collect his benefits. As he was walking down the road, he heard a voice shouting behind him saying, 'Weirdo, you look really stupid'. Because of this, Calvin went home, believing that people were following him meaning to do him harm. When he later discussed what had happened with his psychologist, they were able to complete an evidence list. (You might like to turn back earlier in the chapter to see what they wrote down.) Again after completing this process, Calvin and his psychologist then tried to find an alternative or balanced view that summed up all of the evidence he had collected. They began by summarizing their findings, and then tried to write out a balanced view. At the end of this process, Calvin was asked to rate his belief in this new balanced thought, his belief in his original thought and to re-rate his anxiety.

As you can see, this exercise led both Cath and Calvin to reduce their belief in their troublesome thought and, as a consequence, they both experienced a reduction in anxiety. If you have followed this exercise yourself, hopefully your experience will have been similar. Whether or not this has been the case, we will do more to evaluate your thoughts.

Evidence supporting the thought	Evidence **NOT** supporting the thought
The voices called me a weirdo and said I looked stupid. They've done this before.	No one was behind me and nothing bad has ever happened even though I have had these worries for years and years. I have worried that people think I'm a weirdo, so the voices might be related to my own thoughts.
The balanced view: Although I hear the voices calling me a weirdo and saying I looked stupid, there was no one there. I have had such experiences in the past and worried about them a lot, but no one has ever tried to harm me following these voices. I am worried that people will think I am a weirdo and these voices might be related to my own thoughts since they reflect my own worries.	
Belief in the balanced thought: 60% *Belief in the anxious thought*: 25% *Anxiety now*: 30%	

Earlier in this book we explained that, by changing the way in which we make sense of things, we could change the way that we feel and the way that we behave. This chapter has taken you through the beginning of this process, so now is a good time to ask whether the exercises we have gone through have made a difference to how you feel. If the answer to this question is 'yes', then the following material will help you increase your chances of future success. If, on the other hand, what we have done so far has not been helpful, then we need to find out why not and whether there are any alternative strategies that might be useful.

The focus of the work we have done so far has been the way in which we interpret situations. We have been through a series of steps, which have allowed us to evaluate whether our original interpretations are accurate when we take a balanced view of all the available evidence. Hopefully, you found that developing alternative ways of seeing things by reviewing the evidence is a useful process, allowing you to see that your initial thoughts about a situation are not always the most balanced or accurate view possible. You may have found that this can be achieved most easily when you stand back from a situation, rather than when you are stressed.

It is possible that there are a number of things that you may be finding difficult. The most common ones are:

⊙ You actually don't want to generate alternatives.
⊙ You are unable to remember to generate alternatives.

- Although you remember to generate alternatives you can't actually think of any.
- Even if you manage to generate alternatives none of them seem to be correct, and your previous belief seems to be the most likely.

Let us look at each of these difficulties in turn.

You don't want to generate alternatives

One reason why you might be reluctant to generate alternatives is that you do not have much faith in this process. This could be for a number of reasons. You may have been told that your beliefs are caused by an illness, for example, schizophrenia, which is a biological condition, and that your troublesome thoughts are therefore the result of chemical changes in your brain. If you agree with this viewpoint, it would not be surprising if you felt sceptical about the value of a psychological approach.

A metaphor may be helpful here. For a moment, think of your brain as a computer. A computer has certain fixed components such as wires, the processor chips and keyboard. But it also needs software (instructions or 'programs' that tell it what to do) in order to function. A computer can go wrong in many different ways, as anyone who owns one will know. Obviously, its physical components can be broken, for example as a result of being dropped on the floor. However, it is much more common for the software to become corrupted in some way, distorting the way in which the computer processes information. The wiring and connections have not changed, but the way the computer makes use of information may change so dramatically that it starts producing nonsense or even stops working altogether.

The biological model of schizophrenia assumes that there is a problem with our wiring and that medication helps to fix this. A psychological way of understanding these problems, on the other hand, acknowledges that the problem may not be caused by some kind of physical malfunctioning of the brain, but by the rules (the software) that the brain is trying to follow. In a computer, software can be corrupted by an error in the way the computer program was originally constructed, or by a computer virus arriving over the Internet. In the human brain, 'software' problems can arise because we accidentally learn to see the world in a distorted way, or because our thinking is affected by distressing events. The approach we are describing in this book aims to help with this process.

If you have doubts about what we are suggesting, it may help to list the pros and cons of this approach. After all, what do you have to lose?

Benefits of trying this approach	Problems with trying this approach

You find it difficult to remember to generate alternatives

You may find that you have difficulties remembering to generate alternatives or look at the evidence for your thoughts. When people are in stressful situations, they often forget what they learn and respond automatically, forgetting new information they have recently learned. You may find that your worries and concerns take over, and you are unable to think about what you have read because you are so preoccupied with these worries and concerns. These are extremely common and normal responses.

If this is the case then there may be strategies you could use in order to prevent this from happening. Try to find a way to plan this activity into your day or to generate some reminders that will help you to remember what to do next time you are anxious, angry or feel depressed. Perhaps you could stick a reminder (maybe one of the work sheets) on the inside of a cupboard door (perhaps in the kitchen where you keep your mugs or tea bags) or try to sit down with this workbook for 20 minutes at the same time everyday, perhaps before your lunch or dinner.

Although you remember to generate alternatives, you can't actually think of any

Working with a therapist, you might be thinking something like, 'Well, sat here now with you in the safety of this room, I can begin to think of lots of reasons why I should not believe my anxious thoughts, but when I am elsewhere it is as though I am unable to help myself and the only thing that comes into my mind is that people are looking at me and they are going to harm me in some way.'

The experience described above can be a very common one, especially in the early stages of adopting this approach, when you are just beginning to learn how to apply these strategies. Do not be surprised to find that, at the times when you are calm and relaxed, you are able to recall a situation clearly and then bring to mind a range of different alternative thoughts that could also explain a troubling event. In a relaxed environment you may also be able to evaluate the likelihood of these thoughts and be able to come up with a realistic alternative based on a review of available evidence as described in previous chapters. However, despite this, you may still have some difficulty when you find yourself in a situation that you find stressful.

Many people report that they find the process of generating alternative beliefs fairly easy once they have come out of a situation but, when in the situation itself, find it extremely hard to do this. This often happens in social situations or in public spaces, for example when walking along a busy road or using public transport. At times like this you may find that your mind goes blank. If this happens, there are a number of things you can try.

It might be useful to prepare a list of useful questions, like the ones given earlier in this chapter, to help you generate evidence to challenge your anxious thoughts. You can then keep these questions on a piece of paper in your wallet or purse and get them out when you feel distressed about something and need to generate alternative beliefs. An alternative would be to record these questions onto an audiotape and then play them to yourself on a personal Walkman when you are in one of these difficult situations.

Another strategy, if common themes emerge, would be to generate a list of alternative beliefs when you are feeling calm and relaxed, or with the help of someone else, such as a therapist. As described in previous chapters, these beliefs could be generated and subsequently rated in terms of how much you believe them and how they make you feel. This list could be kept in your wallet or purse and brought out when you require it. Again as described above, audiotaping this information can be useful for some people and may be something you wish to consider. These simple strategies can help you to overcome the problem of being able to recall alternatives when in a difficult situation.

It is important to remember that you are learning. All new skills take time to learn. But as we learn new skills and become better at them, they become easier and more automatic.

For example, most of us take the process of walking for granted. We do not think about how we will walk from one place to another, how we will lift our feet, how high we should lift them; we do all of these things automatically. We learnt these skills over a period of time and now forget the details of them. However, faced with a really tricky situation such as having to walk down a steep and icy path, we may suddenly become extremely aware of the process of walking once more, which enables us to take special care. Similarly, the process of learning new thinking skills is time-consuming at first, takes practice and can be quite difficult. As time goes on, however, we will begin to use these skills without really noticing them, until we encounter a particularly challenging situation, in which case we may have to take notice of them again.

You can think of alternative thoughts, but they don't seem plausible, and your original anxious thought seems to be the best explanation of your experiences.

If this is the case, then the implication is that your initial thought might make the most sense of the evidence you have available. In these circumstances it is important to ensure that you have collected all of the available evidence and not overlooked anything.

Sometimes people say that they are capable of generating and evaluating alternative beliefs, but that even when they do, they still find that their original thought seems to be the more plausible. Of course, if all of the evidence supports your initial belief, then there is a serious possibility that it is the most reasonable explanation of what has been happening to you. (For example, people sometimes really are the victims of conspiracies, although this is not very common.) If you think this might be the case, it is important to check that you are not somehow discounting some important evidence in favour of an alternative explanation. Sometimes beliefs that we have held for a long time can influence the way in which we selectively attend to some kinds of information and ignore other kinds. This can mean that we only notice evidence that fits our beliefs. Often people who are in this situation find that, if they persist with the approach and keep trying to generate alternative explanations, the alternatives gradually begin to appear more plausible.

If you have gone through this process and you still feel that your initial belief best fits the available data, then some problem-solving may be required. For example, many people describe feelings of paranoia that come and go depending on their situation. Sometimes being a bit paranoid can be a useful strategy. For example, if you live in an area with a high crime rate, concerns about your own safety and the safety of your property are perfectly understandable. In these circumstances, feelings of paranoia may prompt you to make sure your property is fully secure and to be careful when you leave your home. Although these strategies may keep you safe, however, they will not solve your problems on their own, and nor will generating alternative beliefs. Clearly, a better strategy would be to find some way of moving to a less threatening neighbourhood or developing a community scheme like a neighbourhood watch association.

This final observation prompts us to repeat an important point. When we advocate generating alternative thoughts, we do not assume that the alternative thoughts will always be more rational and accurate than the anxious thoughts that preceded them. Often they are more rational and accurate, but this is not inevitably so. *The only way of seeing which thoughts are most accurate is by reaching a balanced understanding of all of the available evidence.*

CHAPTER 6

Evaluating your thoughts by changing your behaviour

As we have discovered in previous chapters, Calvin's voices often say unpleasant things to him. At times like this, Calvin understandably adopts certain ways of behaving in order to try to protect himself from the voices and the things that he fears will happen. He will usually go out wearing baggy clothes and a big hood in the hope that the people he worries about will not recognize him, and, therefore, that he will not be attacked. If he sees people that he is worried about, he will usually try to stare them out in order to discourage them from attacking him. When the voices talk about ending up in hospital again, Calvin feels very scared because of his negative experiences of hospital in the past, so he does things to prevent this from happening: for example, he may take extra medication, lie down and try to go to sleep or try to distract himself from what the voices are saying. Calvin believes that he must act on these voices because he feels that they are extremely powerful and fears the consequences of what might happen if he does not do what they say.

The last chapter described how some of these ways of coping might not be as useful as they might initially seem. In this chapter we will look at ways in which you can start to test out the accuracy of some of your beliefs and also find out whether the behaviours in which you engage are useful or counterproductive. This will introduce us to a method of testing these things out by designing experiments, which is another important part of cognitive therapy [19, 20, 23, 24].

As we discussed in Chapter 5, it can sometimes be hard to feel confident in an alternative point of view, especially when we are stressed or in a difficult situation. When we find ourselves with this kind of problem, our experiments will help us to gather information, which we can then use to evaluate our beliefs. In this chapter we will discuss the best way to set up experiments, and how to get the most from them.

WHAT DO YOU WANT TO FIND OUT?

Perhaps the first thing to consider when designing an experiment is to look at what it is that we want to find out. This may seem like a statement of the obvious, but it is a very important first step in designing an experiment. Let us consider the beliefs of Cath and Calvin:

Nous aidons les familles à y faire face

La schizophrénie touche non seulement la personne individuelle, mais aussi toute sa famille.

A REASON TO HOPE. THE MEANS TO COPE.
THE SCHIZOPHRENIA SOCIETY OF ONTARIO
SOCIÉTÉ ONTARIENNE DE LA SCHIZOPHRÉNIE
UNE SOURCE D'ESPOIR, DE SOUTIEN ET D'ENTRAIDE.

Chapitre d'Ottawa

Société ontarienne de la schizophrénie
a/s Centre de santé mentale Royal Ottawa
Pièces 2359 et 2362
1145, avenue Carling
Ottawa (Ontario) K1Z 7K4
Tél. : 613.722.6521 – 7775 et 7776
Fax : 613.729.8980
www.schizophrenia.on.ca
sdeighton@schizophrenia.on.ca

Organisme de bienfaisance no 1 2990 4058 RR0001

Les éléments fondamentaux ... une personne atteinte de sch... mois, de septembre à mai.
- Prise de **médicaments** ... ntale Royal Ottawa, de prévenir les rechutes
- **Éducation** pour aide les pe... schiophrénie et les familles a... pas besoin d'être seul apprivoiser le stress et faire ... ves de la vie. Appelez notre complications qu'elle entraîn... ion sur nos groupes de
- La **réhabilitation psychoso...** collectivité et reprendre la for...

Les gens atteints de schizoph... ...estiné aux personnes atteintes
les symptômes suivants : ...l'humeur ou d'autres formes
- délires ...améliore considérablement la
- entendre des voix imaginaires ...en leur donnant la possibilité n'existent pas ...ruire et de faire des activités
- méfiance et paranoïa ...tuellement. Le Groupe
- difficulté à organiser sa pensée ...upart du temps le mercredi au
- manque de motivation ...munautaires de Carlington,
- indifférence au monde qui les ento... ...a, de 19 h à 21 h.

Où trouver de l'aide? Parlez-en à ...et de livres et vidéos sur les communiquez avec la Société de la sc... rénie, troubles de l'humeur, etc.) là pour vous aider. Nous sommes un o... ources pour les patients et leur famille et nous savons ce que c'est que ...ntale Royal Ottawa. schizophrénie.

Nous vous offrons: ...n, des bénévoles sont à votre
- du soutien pour votre famille ...er aux groupes communautaires,
- des réunions d'information où des spé... ...tablissements d'enseignement. parler de schizophrénie
- de l'information sur les services et pro... ...nous à vous aider. communautaires ...mbre du Chapitre d'Ottawa
- de la camaraderie ...ntarienne de la schizophrénie.
- des conférenciers pour des séances d'éd... ...appel téléphonique suffit! des publications locales, provinciales et n... (après règlement des frais d'adhésion).

...re au Chapitre d'Ottawa de la Société
Comment s'aider soi-même... Chacun e... ...phrénie. problèmes personnels de temps dans la vie. C... qui souffre de schizophrénie peut être un trè... ...5 $ (Famille) voilà pourquoi il est important de vous inscri... ...0 $ (Membre associé) membre. En parler à d'autres personnes qui ont vécu les mêmes situations peuvent vous aid... les difficultés du présent et à vous prémunir dé... **Nous sommes tous avec vous.**

_____ Code postal : _____

...otre chèque à l'ordre du Trésorier SOS. ...st sur la première page de cette brochure.

Schizophrenia Society of Ontario

We Help Families

Schizophrenia affects families as well as individuals

A REASON TO HOPE. THE MEANS TO COPE.
THE SCHIZOPHRENIA SOCIETY OF ONTARIO
SOCIÉTÉ ONTARIENNE DE LA SCHIZOPHRÉNIE
UNE SOURCE D'ESPOIR, DE SOUTIEN ET D'ENTRAIDE.

Ottawa Chapter

Schizophrenia Society of Ontario
c/o Royal Ottawa Mental Health Centre
1145 Carling Avenue
Rooms 2359 & 2362
Ottawa, Ontario K1Z 7K4
Tel: 613.722.6521 ext. 7775 & 7776
Fax: 613.729.8980
www.schizophrenia.on.ca
sdeighton@schizophrenia.on.ca

Charitable Organization No. 1 2990 4058 RR0001

...ical brain disease that can cause

...lic **Information Meetings.**
...rth Tuesday of most months, September to May.
...ditorium, Royal Ottawa Mental Health Centre,
...00-9:00 p.m.

Support Groups. All of life's challenges need not be met on one's own. Call our office for information on Support Groups or visit our Web site.

Friendship Support Group. For people suffering with schizophrenia, mood disorders or other mental illness. Our Friendship Support Group markedly improves the quality of life of its members by giving them the chance to socialize, learn, interact and provide mutual support. The Group meets most Wednesdays at the Carlington Community & Health Services Centre, 900 Merivale Road, Ottawa, 7:00-9:00 p.m.

Library services of books and videos on mental illnesses (schizophrenia, mood disorders, etc.) are available at the Patient & Family Resource Centre, Royal Ottawa Mental Health Centre.

Speakers Bureau. Volunteers are available to speak to community groups, associations and educational institutions upon request.

Help us help you.
Become a member of the Ottawa Chapter,
Schizophrenia Society of Ontario.
We're just a phone call away!

Yes, I would like to join the Ottawa Chapter of the Schizophrenia Society of Ontario.

❏ Membership fee: $35 (Family)
❏ Membership fee: $50 (Associate Member)
❏ Donations: _____

Please print:
Name: _____
Address: _____
City: _____ Postal Code: _____
Tel.: _____
E-Mail: _____

Please make your cheque payable to the Treasurer, SSO. Our address is on the front of this brochure.

Cath has beliefs that the police are out to get her and her conviction in these beliefs fluctuates depending on what is happening in her life.

Calvin believes that he hears the voices of people who want to attack him.

These may look fairly simple on the face of things, but actually these beliefs can be quite difficult to test. Similarly setting up an experiment to prove the existence of ghosts, aliens or the Loch Ness monster may also prove quite difficult. After all, people have been attempting to prove or disprove the existence of these things for many years, spending huge amounts of money in the process. Importantly, even if people find no signs of ghosts or the Loch Ness monster, some people will resist the idea that they do not exist, blaming the outcome on aspects of the experiment, perhaps claiming that the equipment was not good enough, or that if they had looked for longer or perhaps in a different way, then they would have found the evidence they had hoped for. There are two important lessons from these observations. First, we should be careful in deciding which beliefs we want to test by experiment. Second, in order to fairly conduct an experiment to test a belief, we should specify at the beginning of the experiment what kind of evidence will support the belief and what kind of evidence will count against it.

In practice, several different kinds of experiments may be possible.

Surveys

We saw that Cath believes that the police and social services are trying to have her prosecuted. We also saw that testing this belief directly is likely to be difficult. However, what we could do is to try to 'survey' people who Cath trusts, in the hope that she will find their opinions helpful.

Cath decided that she would use the idea of an experiment to see if it was likely that the police were actually spying on her. She decided that she would go to the police station and ask them. So Cath went to the local police station to ask if they were conducting an experiment on her and they said no. Cath decided that they were probably lying and that she couldn't trust them and that, actually, what the police said probably confirmed her fears, as it seemed as if they were trying to cover something up.

If we had considered carefully what we already know about Cath and the way she thinks about things, we could probably have predicted what the outcome of this experiment would have been. Cath was likely to discount the information she obtained from the police because she already mistrusted them.

   Therefore an alternative approach would be to see whether Cath could identify any people in her life that she does trust. She could then ask this group of people questions about what she thinks is happening to her. Before the experiment, she would need to consider how much she trusts these people and whether she would be prepared to consider their opinions. Then it may be useful to ask some questions in a standard way in order to get some information from them. For example, Cath's questions might be the following, presented to trusted people in the form of a short questionnaire:

Do you think it is likely that the police are spying on me? (mark the line below with an X)

0 (Not at all)   100% (Definitely)
_____

How much do you believe that the police and social services target women in order to prosecute them once their children have left home?

0 (Not at all)   100% (Definitely)
_____

I have thought that the police and social services were trying to have my children taken off me for the last 12 years. If this was the case, do you think they would have done something by now?

0 (Not at all) 100% (Definitely)
_____

Could you tell me what kinds of things you think would lead the police and social services to prosecute parents?

1.
2.
3.
4.
5.

Of course, we may not have many people around us who we feel we can trust. A way round this may be to ask other people attending services, for example outpatient or drop-in clinics, to complete this type of survey. If you are working with a therapist, they could offer to ask their colleagues to complete the survey on your behalf. However, if there is no one suitable, then this method is not particularly useful.

EXPERIMENTS

Although it might be difficult to test Cath's belief that the police are spying on her directly, it might be possible to test some of the evidence that she thinks supports the belief. For example:

Cath believes that the police and social services let themselves into her house if she goes out and that they rearrange items in her house in order to remind her that they are watching her.

It might be quite easy for Cath to try to seek evidence about whether or not household items are rearranged in her absence, as she expects. For example, she could note where certain objects are before leaving the house and then check whether they have been moved on returning. Below is the result of Cath's own attempts to test her belief. The design of the experiments, likely problems and the results of the experiments are all filled in on an experiment recording sheet, which we have based on the similar form in Padesky and Greenberger's book *Mind Over Mood* [20]. A blank version of this sheet can be found in the Appendix at the back of the book, in case you want to devise your own experiments.

A survey could also be useful in relation to Cath's worries about things being moved. For example, her therapist asked their colleagues if they ever have the feeling that something in their own house has been moved, when they do not have an explanation for it. Eight out of eleven people said that they had experienced this feeling, with six of them saying it happened often; this also made Cath feel less concerned.

One of the difficulties with testing Cath's belief above is the experiment that was used to test it. Checking everything in the house in order to see if anything has moved is likely to unearth something with an original location that cannot be clearly recalled. This uncertainty might lead us to believe that maybe it has moved. Therefore it might be better if Cath changed her own behaviour – for example, by going outside without looking at the pavement and counting – to see what happens. This type of test is known as *a behavioural experiment*.

BEHAVIOURAL EXPERIMENTS

In this section we will discuss how to test our beliefs by changing our safety behaviours. Remember that, although these kinds of behaviours

Thought to be tested: The police come into my house and move things when I am out

Belief in thought: (0–100%) Before experiment 100%   **After experiment** 95%

Experiment to test thought	Likely problems	Strategies to deal with problems	Expected outcome	Actual outcome	Alternative thought
Go out of the house and on my return check to see if certain items have been moved. Gas bill lined up with the right edge of the kitchen table, touching lamp. Footstool tucked under dining room table. Shopping basked on sofa. Photograph album on bedside table.	I may not be able to accurately remember where every single thing in the house is. If I look for things that may have moved, it is possible that I might find it. Someone else may have come into the house and moved things	If the police are doing it on purpose they will most likely move things that I will notice, so I should only focus on certain things. Put my burglar alarm on. Leave the dog in. Go out with someone else like my daughter.	Things will be moved.	The things I had identified did not seem to have moved and my daughter was convinced that these things had not moved. The alarm had not gone off and the dog appeared settled when we got back.	It did not seem as though anyone had been in on this occasion.

can make us feel better in the short term, in the long term they might actually be making us feel worse.

The first thing to do is to highlight which behaviour we want to change and then how we want to test it. Your answers to the exercise at the end of the last chapter (particularly to the question: Do I do anything to stop these things from happening?) should help you identify suitable behaviours.

As we have seen, Calvin has been experiencing voices for a number of years. He is unsure whose they are (although one of them sounds very similar to the person who abused him when he was in care). When the voice tells him to 'Stick up for yourself' or says 'He is talking about you, go and hit him', Calvin feels compelled to do what it says. He feels that he has no option but to obey these commands and that something awful will happen to him if he does not. He thinks that the voices are extremely powerful.

Calvin was clear that he did not want to get rid of the voices altogether because they would sometimes provide him with comfort. However, he did want to feel more in control of them. Calvin believed that, at present, he had no control over the voices whatsoever, they were extremely powerful, happened for no reason at all and came out of the blue.

An experiment was therefore designed to see if Calvin was able to influence his voices, and to see if he could gain some control over them. Because he initially believed that he had no control over them whatsoever, he was taught ways of bringing them on (thinking about the time when he was in care seemed to be a useful way of bringing them on) and also strategies for reducing their severity (reading from a book and listening to music seemed to temporarily block them out). Calvin was then asked to experiment with these strategies and the results are shown in the first of the following experiment sheets.

Calvin was also under the impression that other people could hear his voices. He became embarrassed about them and would isolate himself (as a safety behaviour), partly because he was worried that people may hear some of the nasty things they were saying. He was clear that sometimes the voices were not very loud but sometimes they were and other people would be sure to hear them. Again an experiment was set up to test out this belief and the results can be seen in the second sheet.

As can be seen from these experiments, testing things out in a structured way can be extremely useful. It may be helpful to think about how you could use experiments to test out some ideas of your own troublesome thoughts. Use the experiment sheet in the Appendix to identify some potential thoughts and behaviours to test, but remember to think about potential problems and ways that you could deal with these problems.

Doing these experiments made Calvin feel safe enough to try to stop his safety behaviours. The next time he heard his voices when he was in a public place he stayed there (rather than going home) and found out that

Thought to be tested: The voices I hear are not under my control

Belief in thought: (0–100%) Before experiment 100%   **After experiment** 30%

Experiment to test thought	Likely problems	Strategies to deal with problems	Expected outcome	Actual outcome	Alternative thought
Attempt to bring on the voices by thinking about my earlier life and then use strategies to reduce the voices.	I may not be able to bring on voices or reduce them. I may get upset when the voices start.	To practise these techniques whilst in therapy session so that there is someone available to help.	I will not be able to bring on the voice or get rid of them.	Within a short span of time I was able to bring on the voice by thinking about certain things. I was able to stop them when I was doing the reading, although this was only for a short time.	Perhaps I have some control over the voices and they are not as powerful as I thought.

Thought to be tested: Other people can hear my voices

Belief in thought: (0–100%) Before experiment 100% | **After experiment** 20%

Experiment to test thought	Likely problems	Strategies to deal with problems	Expected outcome	Actual outcome	Alternative thought
Bring on the voices in session and use a tape recorder to record what is going on in the room. Have a radio playing in the background so that I can check that the tape recorder is working.	Not sure of any.		The tape recorder will hear the voices and they will probably be as loud as the radio.	Could not hear anything except the radio. The voices were not that loud, but they were at least as loud as the radio we had playing so we should have heard them.	Perhaps other people cannot hear the voices. I will look at other people's reactions next time I hear them and see if they react rather than isolating myself.

people did not seem to be hearing the voices. The next time that the voices told him he was going to be attacked by someone, he again stayed where he was and did not try to stare them out. He found out that he was not attacked, and this made him feel less anxious and helped him to re-evaluate his beliefs about people wanting to harm him.

EXPERIMENT SHEET

Thought to be tested:

Belief in thought: (0–100%) Before experiment

Experiment to test thought	Likely problems	Strategies to deal with problems	After experiment		
			Expected outcome	Actual outcome	Alternative thought

Helpful and unhelpful ways of coping

In this chapter we will consider how you might improve your ability to cope with your problems. Sensibly, people tend to develop their own methods of coping and these strategies can often be some of the most useful and meaningful [25]. Usually, they are developed gradually, over a long period of time, as people accidentally discover that certain actions or behaviours seem to make things either better or worse. In the fullness of time, these evolve into clear coping strategies that are used, often in the absence of help from health care professionals. Examples may include things like adjusting diet to avoid too much tea or coffee, listening to soothing music, or seeking solitude. However, as we have discussed throughout this book, sometimes the things we do that are designed to help us cope with our problems end up keeping the problems going. In some cases, they may actually make the problems worse.

Calvin was becoming increasingly tired, he was finding it harder to get to sleep and would find himself up late into the night playing video games or watching television. To compensate for this Calvin would allow himself to sleep until late in the day, sometimes not getting up till 4.00 or 5.00 pm. As a consequence, he was unable to attend his college course. He was very keen to attend this course as he had tried to get a place on it for a number of years. When he didn't go it made him feel worse. He worried what the tutor would say about his absence, and this would then play on his mind when he was trying to get to sleep.

As we can see, this strategy (allowing himself to sleep in) was designed to help Calvin cope with feeling tired. In some ways, the strategy could even be regarded as successful in the short term, as it helped him overcome his tiredness. However, the problem was that Calvin had allowed a short-term strategy to become a way of coping in the long term. It is easy to see why it was hard for Calvin to break out of this vicious circle, once it was established. Because he woke so late in the day, he was even less inclined to go to sleep at a sensible time at night. In the end, the normal rhythm of waking and sleeping was almost reversed. A coping strategy that worked at first had become problematic.

In this chapter we will help you to identify your current coping strategies and see how useful they really are. We will help you to work out whether your current strategies could be improved in any way, or see whether, on the contrary, they should be stopped because they are now causing more harm than good.

In the past Calvin had experienced voices when he had been alone in the house. He has responded to these critical voices by shouting back them at them. This way of coping with his voices reduced some of his frustration and stopped him being able to hear them for a while. However, his neighbours felt threatened by his shouting and have complained to the police. When the police arrived at Calvin's door in order to investigate the complaint, Calvin felt stressed and frightened.

Calvin's psychologist asked him to consider other methods of coping that he had used in the past and this reminded him that he used to listen to music when he was distressed, and that reading also seemed to reduce the voices in the short term. Listening to music had helped him a lot, but he had stopped when his stereo system had broken down some time ago. Calvin decided to spend a small amount of money to repair his stereo and to invest in a pair of headphones. He agreed to try to listen to music through his headphones if he started to experience the voices during the next week. He was also asked to keep a record of:

> How often he heard the voices.
> How distressed this made him.
> What he did.
> How often his neighbours called the police.

When Calvin tried his new strategy, he found that, although he still experienced his voices, they did not last as long as they had done previously and that he was not as distressed by them. He also found that if he listened to music or tried reading a magazine instead of shouting, then the neighbours no longer complained to the police. He, therefore, felt less stressed and his relationship with his neighbours improved.

Coping strategies can vary tremendously from person to person and strategies that some people find helpful can be problematic for others. The secret is to see what works for *you* but also to learn from others what has helped them.

Coping strategies fall into a number of different categories:

⊙ Coping with psychosis.
⊙ Coping with the stigma associated with mental health problems.
⊙ Coping with everyday life.

Calvin evaluated his coping strategies by filling in the following questionnaire:

What do you do to cope?	Helpful aspects of this strategy	Unhelpful aspects of this strategy	What have you learnt?
Shout at the voices	Makes me feel better at the time Gets my anger out	Neighbours complain Police are usually called They make me more angry I get more stressed	Distraction may be a useful alternative rather than responding to the voices by shouting at them when at home in the flat. Try to distract myself by using strategies such as listening to music through my headphones, reading a magazine or watching a film that I would enjoy.
Smoke cannabis	Makes me feel less stressed by the voices	The voices tend to go on for longer I can feel more paranoid when I have had a smoke	Perhaps it might be worth trying to go out.
Go to bed	Not sure, just something I have always tended to do	Hear the voices Feel alone and depressed	
Listen to music	This can distract me from my voices Feel calmer The police don't come round if I use my headphones	I have to listen to something fairly loud to distract me	

COPING WITH PSYCHOSIS

Throughout this book we have focused on the idea of developing strategies for managing the distress associated with psychosis on the assumption that once the distress is reduced, psychotic experiences will tend to improve. Some of the techniques we have suggested, such as evaluating our thoughts, can also be used when we are feeling upset, angry or sad. Many people also find that psychiatric drugs can be helpful, and we will discuss the benefits and costs of these drugs in a later chapter. However, it can also be important to try to remember our ambitions and dreams and ensure that we continue to strive towards achieving these.

Recovery can be a gradual process and it is important to remember that setbacks can happen and, indeed, are to be expected. It is unusual for someone to get steadily better and better without encountering obstacles. It is more likely that, for every two steps forward you find yourself taking one step back. When this step back occurs it can feel as if you are back at square one, but this is very rarely the case. When setbacks occur, we need to remember that overall progress is still in the right direction. Below is a typical graph depicting how recovery occurs.

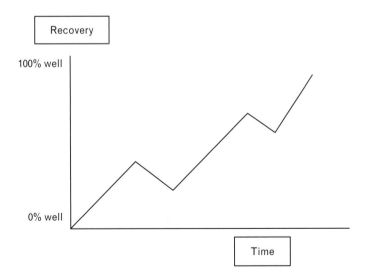

COPING WITH THE STIGMA ASSOCIATED WITH MENTAL HEALTH PROBLEMS

Many people find that the stigma associated with mental health problems leaves them feeling isolated and prevents them from socializing with others. They worry about what other people will think of them and this prevents them from engaging with others. You may be able to get help with this problem from your mental health team. However, many people have found that having access to others who have been through similar experiences is particularly helpful. User and self-help groups can be a useful way of sharing experiences, and forming relationships with others who will have had similar experiences, in a non-threatening environment. Also, it can be useful to remember that many people (including famous people such as artists, actors and musicians) have psychotic experiences but do not need any contact with mental health services (it may be helpful to look at Chapter 2 again).

COPING WITH EVERYDAY LIFE

Everyday life can be hard enough at times, but for someone who has extra difficulties, managing even the most simple of everyday tasks can sometimes feel daunting. Don't be afraid to ask for help with tasks that may feel beyond you. It may be that you haven't had the opportunity to develop skills in managing your life. Perhaps, because of your difficulties, you have missed out on the opportunity to learn ordinary, everyday tasks. (Our experience is that people who develop psychotic problems in adolescence sometimes find themselves living with their parents well into adulthood, so that they do not get the chance to try living independently until much later than most.) If this is the case, help may be available from occupational therapy services, or from courses provided at a local college.

ALTERNATIVE COPING STRATEGIES

It is important to develop a wide range of coping strategies. Throughout the book we have focused on cognitive strategies (strategies that involve finding the best way of thinking about things). However it may be helpful to think about other approaches. Think about things such as diet and exercise – poor eating habits and lack of exercise can lead to lethargy and fatigue, mimicking many of the symptoms of depression. Are you getting a varied diet? Are you getting enough exercise? Scientific studies have consistently shown that graded exercise can improve alertness and mood – in fact, in many studies exercise turned out to be just as effective as antidepressant drugs (but without the side effects).

If you have an unhealthy diet and take no exercise, it may be helpful to think about how you could incorporate a better diet into your life or begin to develop a programme of exercise. If you have not exercised for a long time, it is important to start gradually. It is also important to expect some soreness afterwards, at least at first. Typically, unused muscles that are experiencing exercise for the first time will become stiff and ache soon after exercise, and these feelings will build up over time, usually peaking the day afterwards. It is therefore important to realize that, if you feel uncomfortable the day after exercising, this is perfectly normal, and certainly not a sign that anything has gone wrong.

You can begin to improve your physical fitness without going anywhere near a gym. You could start to walk to certain places instead of relying on public transport or lifts. Doctors recommend that people should have half an hour of aerobic exercise (exercise that raises your pulse rate) at least three times a week, and a brisk walk is sufficient for this purpose. However, formal exercise classes of one sort or another are widely available. Gym membership can be quite expensive, but you may find that very inexpensive classes are available at local leisure centres and similar venues. Swimming is an excellent form of aerobic exercise, and also usually inexpensive.

Sometimes people avoid exercise because they think that it will make them feel too tired. Exercise may make you feel tired at first but after only a short period of regular exercise it has exactly the opposite effect. We do not have a fixed amount of energy to spend – amazingly, the more we spend the more we get! As your fitness improves you will find yourself more alert, more motivated and able to tackle more demands on your life.

We know of a lot of people who have taken up yoga, reporting that it has helped not only in terms of exercise, but also by helping them develop good mental coping strategies. Some people find that simple steps like reducing caffeine by limiting tea and coffee can be extremely beneficial. Many people have found that limiting the amount of street drugs they take can have a profound and beneficial effect on the way they feel. In general, street drugs can be quite harmful for people with psychosis (we say this without wishing to appear judgemental). There is now very good scientific evidence that drugs such as cannabis, amphetamine and cocaine (which have powerful effects on the chemistry of the brain) can precipitate episodes of psychosis in people who are vulnerable [26]. Unfortunately, people with psychosis often take these drugs in an attempt to improve their feelings of unhappiness or despondency but, in the long term, the effects are almost always the opposite. In fact, taking street drugs can be considered another example of a coping strategy that seems beneficial in the short term (people with psychotic problems who take them often feel happier for a while), but that in the long term can be damaging. There is no getting away from the fact that street drugs will tend to make psychotic problems persist.

It can be important to have good things in your life, things that you can look forward to in both the short and the longer term. Positive experiences at regular intervals are vital to keep us feeling energetic and optimistic about the future. Positive experiences can be as simple as going down to the pub, kicking around a football with friends, a visit to the cinema or planning a weekend away to look forward to. Our experience is that people with psychosis often feel unable to indulge themselves in these ways for a variety of reasons. Their psychotic problems sometimes get in the way (they are too frightened to go to the pub), they do not feel that they deserve pleasurable experiences, they think that those kinds of experiences should be put off until they have achieved something useful, or they feel that they lack the necessary energy to bring them about, or they have simply forgotten how to have a good time. If psychotic problems are the main obstacle, the methods we have already introduced you to in this book should help. Similarly, if you feel that you do not deserve pleasurable experiences, this is probably because of some negative automatic thoughts, which on closer examination will turn out to be open to re-evaluation. Putting off pleasurable experiences indefinitely is almost always a mistake because these experiences give us the motivation to tackle the less pleasurable demands of life (the trick is to get the right balance between self-indulgence and effort on routine tasks). Finally, like exercise, pleasurable activities can bring about increases of energy, more than repaying the efforts made to initiate them. (At some time in your life you will have probably had the experience of making yourself go to a social event of some kind, feeling that you would much rather stay at home and watch the television. If you think back to that time you will probably recall that you enjoyed the event, despite the fact that you had to force yourself to go to it.)

Many people who experience psychosis find that more creative pastimes can be extremely beneficial. These include writing, painting, photography, music, dance or sculpture. In fact, there is good scientific evidence that people with psychotic difficulties are, on average, much more creative than ordinary people, so it makes sense to exploit any creative inclinations that you might have.

Alternative therapies are becoming more and more popular, and some-times people with psychosis turn to these in the hope that they improve their ability to cope with life. While there is no scientific evidence that approaches such as acupuncture, reflexology or massage can help with psychosis, they can sometimes be useful by encouraging relaxation and self-confidence.

Cath had been having some problems with her medication, she was feeling increasingly troubled by side effects, but worried that discussing them with the team might lead them to think that she was becoming ill again. However, she decided to speak to her support worker about the situation. The support worker listened to her worries and wrote them down to ensure that she had understood them properly. Cath agreed with what had been written down and was keen for the support worker to attend her next meeting with the team.

At the team meeting the support worker discussed the difficulties Cath was experiencing. The team listened carefully to the list of problems and decided to reduce her medication to see if this was helpful. Over the next few weeks Cath began to feel much better because the side effects had virtually disappeared. This greatly reduced her stress levels, and the worry she had had about confronting the team. Because she felt less stressed she was able to do more and this made her feel better about herself.

Sometimes small changes in the way we manage difficulties can have a big effect on the way we feel. Consider the strategies you use to manage your difficulties and see if some alternatives could be used, or whether just improving the ones you already use might be helpful. To do this, it might be useful to complete the coping strategies evaluation form, which is in the Appendix.

Feeling good about yourself

It is quite common for people to think negatively about themselves when out and about. Under these circumstances, it is easy to feel anxious or paranoid. Negative beliefs that have been held for a long time may suddenly leap to mind. These beliefs may be about yourself, other people or the world in general.

Beliefs of this kind are often formed early in our lives as the result of difficult or uncomfortable circumstances. Although children are obviously not responsible for the bad things happen that to them, often the only way they can make sense of traumatic events is by blaming themselves. This may happen especially if, for example, children are repeatedly told that they are bad, or if they are consistently treated badly by those who should be caring for them. Under these circumstances, a child can easily assume that bad things happen to them because they are a bad person.

Because these kinds of beliefs develop early in life, it sometimes does not occur to us to question them. Rather, we may accept them as 100% accurate and think, feel and behave as if they are true.

Cath was brought up as the youngest of six children. Her mother was very depressed throughout her childhood and as a result had little time for the children and showed them no affection. Cath's father was very strict and believed that children should live by the rules of their father, do as they are told at all times, and should be punished if at all disobedient. He also believed that rewarding or praising children would make them vain and therefore never did this. At school, Cath was often dressed in ill-fitting, shabby second-hand clothes and would turn up unwashed and without her hair brushed as her mother was too depressed to care for her. As a result, she was bullied throughout school, was called a 'weirdo' and was picked on by staff and pupils alike.

When Cath was 18 she met a man and became pregnant. When her father found out about this he called her a 'slut' and a 'whore', threw her out of the family home and told her not to return. She married because she felt that she had no other options. However, as we have already seen, the marriage was an unhappy one and her husband was every bit as critical towards her as her father had been.

On talking with Cath, her therapist discovered that she had the following beliefs: 'I am bad', 'Other people are better than me', 'People will laugh at me' and 'If others find out how bad I am they will take my children away from mc'. Following the birth of her first child, these beliefs had made her doubt her ability to care for her son and she had become worried that others would find out what a bad mother she was. As we saw in earlier chapters, she had become too afraid to leave the house and had begun to interpret everything in the neighbourhood as a sign that social services and the police were investigating her. Following the birth of her second child, this problem had became so severe that she had become too frightened to visit the nearby shops and had resorted to stealing milk from the doorsteps of neighbouring houses in order to feed her children. Doing this had only added to her feelings of badness, and her worries about what the police might do to her.

When the therapist began working with Cath, it appeared that all her concerns centred on her beliefs that she was bad and unfit to be a mother. Because this belief system had helped Cath to make sense of her world at a very young age, she had never thought to evaluate whether it was a useful or realistic way of looking at herself. Instead, she had accepted her beliefs as 100% true.

In this chapter we will help you to identify any core beliefs that contribute to your distress. We will also help you to understand why such beliefs persist, despite any positive experiences or feedback that you may receive. Whatever the origins of these beliefs, this chapter will help you to change them to more realistic and more helpful ways of thinking about yourself, the world and other people.

WHY DO BELIEFS KEEP THEMSELVES GOING?

Cath had believed 'I am bad', 'I am worthless' and 'I am stupid' since she was very young. These beliefs made sense to her because she had often been told such things at home and school, and her parents had never praised her for anything she did. On questioning, Cath informed her therapist that she believed each of these statements about herself 100%.

Cath's therapist then asked her to consider what she thought when anyone said anything negative about her or acted in a negative way towards her. Cath told her therapist that she would think 'just as I thought' or 'they're right about me'. Her therapist then asked her to consider what she would think if anyone said something positive about her, complimented her or acted in a way that suggested that they thought she was good, worthy or bright. Cath thought about this for a while. She then replied that, if this happened, she would probably ignore the compliment and think it had been made by mistake, or to assume that she was being made fun of.

Cath and her therapist discussed what was happening. It seems that whenever Cath saw or heard anything that fitted with her negative view of herself, she would accept it as truth and store it in her memory as 'evidence' that she was bad, worthless and stupid. On the other hand, if anyone said or did anything that did not fit with Cath's view of herself, she would either ignore this information or change it until it fitted with her beliefs (e.g. by saying to herself 'They're only saying nice things about me to make fun of me because they think I'm stupid and bad').

When we look at Cath's way of thinking, her problems become obvious: Cath both ignores and discounts information that does not fit with her negative beliefs about herself or she squashes it to fit her existing beliefs. This means that however much information is around that contradicts her beliefs, she is never able to use this information to challenge her low opinion of herself. Therefore, irrespective of what other people say or do, what she achieves or what others think of her, Cath continues to believe she is bad, worthless and stupid. In fact, as time passes she is storing more and more 'evidence' of her badness in her memory.

Fortunately, something can be done to reverse this process. In previous chapters we have learned to identify and evaluate thoughts that cause us distress. In this chapter, we will help you to learn how to do this for your core beliefs (those beliefs about yourself that you have held for a very long time). Although these kinds of beliefs are harder and take longer to change than our automatic thoughts, this can be done. This is something that you will need to persist with over a period of weeks or even months rather than hours, but the results will be long lasting and are likely to make a real difference to how you feel. The first thing to do is to identify core beliefs that are causing you problems.

IDENTIFYING CORE BELIEFS

If you take a look at your thought records or, if you hear voices, what they have said over the past few months, you are likely to notice some themes that appear to keep coming up time after time. These themes emerge because the way that we think on a day-to-day basis is very much influenced by our core beliefs about the world, other people and ourselves. Therefore, studying the themes in your thoughts and voices will help you to work out what your core beliefs are.

Cath reviewed what her anxiety-provoking thoughts had been over the past few months. She looked at some of her thought records she had done with her therapist.

Event	Thoughts	Feeling
What happened?	What was going through my mind? What am I worrying is the worst that might happen? What images or memories come to mind in this situation?	What were you feeling? How strong was it 0–100?
Received GP letter	They have found out how bad I am, and will arrest me	Anxious 90
Walking along road, helicopter above	They are watching me. They know I am bad and are trying to get evidence against me	Anxious 85
New neighbour knocks on the door	She seems so nice, but will find out how bad I am and hate me soon	Depressed 70

Can you identify any themes that might indicate Cath's core belief about herself? The theme is: 'I am _____'

When Cath and her therapist reviewed some of her thought records, it appeared that she often thought of herself as bad, and many of the disasters or difficulties that she predicted were because she thought she was bad and that others would eventually find this out and punish her.

Think about some of the thoughts records that you have filled out over recent days or weeks. In Padesky and Greenberger's book *Mind Over Mood* [20], they recommend to people with depression that they try to see if there is a theme running through their thought records, and people with psychotic problems can benefit from taking exactly the same approach. Use the following blank form to write out a few of your negative thoughts in brief and see if you can identify any themes.

Event	Thoughts	Feeling
What happened?	What was going through my mind? What am I worrying is the worst that might happen? What images or memories come to mind in this situation?	What were you feeling? How strong was it 0–100?

Can you spot any obvious themes? Try filling out the questions below once you have completed the thought record.

I am: _____

Others are: _____

The world is: _____

The other way in which we can identify our core beliefs is by further self-questioning (known as the downward arrow technique [20, 21]). Think about the 'hot' thoughts that you arrived at when doing your thought records and continue to ask yourself, 'What might this say about me, others or about the world?'

Think about a thought you identified or a situation in which you felt upset, anxious or angry.

_____

_____

↓

Ask yourself what this might say about me, others or the world?

I am: _____

Others are: _____

The world is: _____

↓

If that is correct, what does this say about you, others or the world?

I am: _____

Others are: _____

The world is: _____

↓

If that is correct, what does this say about you, others or the world?

I am: _____

Others are: _____

The world is: _____

Once you have done this you may have identified some core beliefs that you are ready to test. Do they feel right to you? Do they make sense of how you feel, think and act much of the time? If so, we may be ready to move on to check out these beliefs. If not, try to repeat this (or the previous) exercise a few times until you find some beliefs that feel as if they make sense of some of your thinking, feelings and behaviour.

EVALUATING CORE BELIEFS

As we discussed earlier, although core beliefs are harder and take longer to change than our automatic thoughts, this can be done. This is something that you will need to continue working on over a period of weeks and months rather than hours, but the results will be long lasting and are likely to make a real difference to how you feel.

Earlier we discovered that Cath believed 'I am bad' (amongst other things). She believed this 100%, despite the fact that there were plenty of things that had happened that did not fit with this belief at all. Cath sat down with her therapist whilst she explained the diagram (visible on page 23) that shows how we only 'store' evidence that fits with our negative beliefs and ignore or distort positive information. This explained how Cath might continue to believe that she was bad, despite plenty of evidence to the contrary. Once they had done this, Cath and her therapist decided to review the accuracy of her beliefs and to keep track of all the information that did not fit with them that had previously been ignored or rejected by Cath.

Use the following worksheet, adapted from *Mind Over Mood* [20], to record evidence that does NOT fit 100% with your core belief. Do this over the next few weeks or months. Do this for all of the core beliefs that you identify about yourself, others or the world. (Another copy of the core belief worksheet can be found in the Appendix.)

CORE BELIEF WORKSHEET

Core belief to be tested _____
Write below any evidence that suggests that this core belief is not 100% true at all times. Has someone said or done something that does not fit with your core belief?   Has someone said or done something that suggests that they do not agree with your core belief? Is there anyone who would point out things that do not fit with your core belief? What would they point out?

1.	
2.	
3.	
4.	
5.	
6.	

Cath and her therapist sat down and began to look at evidence that did not fit with her core belief 'I am bad'. She then kept this worksheet for the following couple of months.

Core belief to be tested _____

Write below any evidence that suggests that this core belief is not 100% true at all times. Has someone said or done something that does not fit with your core belief?
Has someone said or done something that suggests that they do not agree with your core belief? Is there anyone who would point out things that do not fit with your core belief? What would they point out?

1.	My daughter tells me that she loves me
2.	I always give money to charities
3.	Last week, on the way to an appointment, a young woman asked me directions. She was upset, as she had been lost for ages; I walked her to the street so she wouldn't get lost again
4.	I've told my therapist all about my past and all the things I've done and she still appears to accept me
5.	Last week the woman at Morrison's thanked me for being so patient whilst she waited for help. She told me it was her first day and I was the only person who had been helpful and understanding that morning
6.	I always try to hold doors for mums with prams, even when I'm feeling really anxious

---

Once you feel more confident in doing this, you may want to think about an alternative, more accurate core belief. Having identified this, you can move to collecting evidence that fits with this 'alternative' core belief, using the form (again based on one from *Mind Over Mood* [20]).

New or 'alternative' belief _____

Write below any evidence that suggests that this new belief is true. Has someone said or done something that fits with this new belief or shows they agree with it? Is there anyone who would point out things that fit with your new core belief? What would they point out?

1.

2.

3.

4.

5.

6.

C H A P T E R 9

Staying well

Calvin had been doing very well. He had not been in hospital since last year. He was becoming more relaxed, had been thinking about reducing his medication and had decided to discuss this possibility with his CPN and his doctor at his next outpatient appointment. However, when he talked to them they were both wary about this idea. They emphasized that Calvin had been really unwell in the past when he had not taken his medication consistently. They said that, because he was doing well, it was important not to do anything that could upset things at the present time. However, they cautiously agreed that a small reduction could be tried, but also stressed that, should Calvin notice any of the symptoms that he had experienced before his previous admission, he should contact them immediately.

Calvin was initially very pleased with the plan but, on reflection, he started to get a bit worried. He kept remembering what he had been told by the doctor and his CPN about how serious his problems were. Over the next few days he found it difficult to get these worries out of his mind and found himself becoming increasingly anxious. As a consequence, he did not sleep very well and then became more suspicious of people in the street. At this stage he recognized these symptoms as being similar to those he had experienced the last time he had been admitted to hospital. On that occasion he had been sectioned and kept in hospital for some time.

Calvin worried further that the symptoms he was experiencing were, in fact, indicators of a relapse and felt confused. Should he tell someone and risk being admitted to hospital, which was something he did not want, or should he try to deal with it himself?

One of the things that people with psychotic experiences tend to worry about is becoming unwell again [27]. This fear can exist for many reasons, but most obviously because people remember awful experiences during a previous psychotic episode. They may remember the extremely frightening experiences and beliefs that they had, the unpleasant treatments for these difficulties (including the distressing side effects of medication), and being forcibly admitted to hospital. Other consequences of becoming unwell may be just as worrying, such as a damaged career or disrupted relationships with friends or family members.

Very often people who have experienced several episodes of psychosis learn to recognize early warning signs that they are becoming unwell.

Changes in mood, behaviour and thoughts usually begin to appear 2–6 weeks prior to a relapse, and this period is known as the *relapse prodrome* [28]. Some typical prodromal symptoms are shown in the table below:

Some typical relapse signs	
Increased tension	Anxiety
Depression	Eating problems
Concentration problems	Sleeping difficulties
Irritability	Becoming suspicious
Mild paranoia	Social withdrawal

It is not surprising that people who have not learned to recognize their prodromal symptoms very often wish to do so; they want to learn about the early warning signs of their difficulties in the hope that this will help them to prevent relapses from happening. Research has shown that people who have experienced episodes of psychosis tend to monitor their own symptoms, and modify their behaviour or lifestyle if they notice any changes [29]. They may engage in diversionary tactics, seek professional help, and resume or increase their medication.

If these early signs and symptoms can be identified, they may present an opportunity for quick action. Treatments aimed at reducing such symptoms, if administered at this stage, may help to prevent a relapse from occurring. Drug treatments have most commonly been used in relapse prevention (usually involving an increase in existing antipsychotic drugs or the prescription of alternative medications, for example antidepressants, that target specific symptoms). Increased monitoring of the person's mental state and increased support are usually also considered. However, a recent research study has shown that cognitive therapy, when delivered to people who were showing early signs of relapse, was effective in reducing actual relapse rates and admissions to hospital [30]. In this study, it was found that the most common thoughts reported by patients who were at risk of relapse are fears of hospitalization and its consequences. The researchers suggest that these anxious thoughts could trigger strong emotions, which, in turn, could further fuel these thoughts, until the whole process spirals out of control. It therefore seems that worries about relapse can cause relapses to occur (another kind of vicious cycle, similar to several others we have already come across in this book).

This kind of vicious cycle can be seen when Calvin began to worry about what his CPN and psychiatrist had said to him:

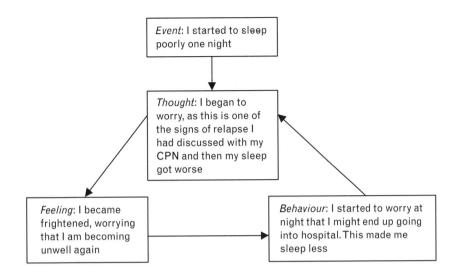

PRACTICAL APPLICATION

Although preventing relapse is an important part of cognitive therapy, it can sometimes prove difficult. Some people will experience relief from the distress of their symptoms after a few sessions and feel no need for further therapy. They may be keen to put their experiences behind them and get on with their lives, which is quite understandable. However, this approach to recovery, in which the recovering person tries not to think about what has happened and just wants to put it in the past, seems to increase the chance of relapse. An alternative approach to recovery involves the person learning as much about psychosis as possible, trying to work out what led to the psychotic experiences, and working to develop strategies that may prevent this from happening again. Interestingly this recovery style can be beneficial, and seems to lead to reduced rates of relapse. If you follow this path, it does not mean that you can never forget about the problems, just that it can be helpful to learn about what happened and what helps.

If you have suffered from a psychotic episode, you can begin this process by thinking about all the possible signs and symptoms, and trying to work out which have happened to you during the initial stages of your last episode. You may want to get someone who knows you well to help with this. Sometimes it can be difficult to remember all of the things that happened to you during this particularly difficult period in your life, so it is a good idea to ask the opinion of someone else who saw what happened. Overleaf is a list of common problems that have been reported by many people and this can be used as a checklist to see whether these happen to you. Once you have gone through the list, try to decide whether there are any other things, which may be very specific to you. For example, it is possible that you start to do certain things, perhaps wearing a particular piece of clothing, listening to a specific piece of music or perhaps attending church when this is something you would not normally do.

Common prodromal symptoms (mark any experienced before last episode):

Talking or smiling to myself	Feeling unable to cope, difficulty in managing everyday tasks and interactions	Having aches and pains	My speech comes out jumbled or is full of odd words	Feeling tired or lacking energy	Feel like playing tricks or pranks
I become preoccupi-ed with one or two things	Feeling quiet and withdrawn	Not feeling like eating	Feeling stubborn or refusing to carry out simple requests	Sleep has been restless or unsettled	Losing my temper easily
Feeling useless or helpless	Feeling violent	Feeling dissatisfied with myself	Feeling as if my thoughts might be controlled	My movements seem slow	Others have difficulty in following what I am saying
Feeling depressed or low	Feeling very excited	Feeling as if I'm being watched	Feeling as if I'm being laughed at or talked about	Feeling confused or puzzled	Feeling aggressive or pushy
Feeling as if my thoughts might not be my own	Thinking I could be someone else	Being open and explicit about sexual matters	Feeling tense afraid or anxious	Having no interest in things	Feeling forgetful or 'far away'
Having difficulty concentrat-ing	Behaving oddly for no reason	Feeling irritable or quick tempered	Not bothered about my appearance or hygiene		

RELAPSE SIGNATURE

Once you have identified all the symptoms that belong to what we will now call your 'relapse signature', these can be placed on a time line indicating when you imagine these things would happen in terms of you becoming unwell again, starting from a couple of months before an episode, leading up to just before you become unwell.

When questioned about his experiences in the eight weeks before his last admission, Calvin told his psychiatrist that he often heard voices and these never really went away. However, when he was fairly well he would not hear these voices very much, and they also did not upset him. During these periods, he was able to get on with his life. So, although he never got rid of all his symptoms, he experienced them a lot less often when he was well, and some difficulties disappeared altogether.

Calvin's voices usually seem to get worse about two weeks before a relapse. However, several weeks before this, he usually becomes anxious, has trouble sleeping and cannot concentrate. These experiences are illustrated on a timeline below.

Because many healthy people experience psychotic states at some point in their lives, these symptoms can be regarded as part of the normal range of human experience. It is important, therefore, to recognize that the development of psychotic experiences does not necessarily herald the onset of a full-blown psychotic episode. Rather, it is unhelpful interpretations of these experiences that can lead to them spiralling out of control.

For example, if Calvin has thoughts like:

I am experiencing these symptoms again! Oh my God, this is what happened last time I became unwell. I bet it's all starting again!

it is likely that he will experience increasing anxiety, and that this will then lead to further difficulties. However, if Calvin is able to consider alternatives such as:

I am experiencing symptoms again and it is possible that I might become unwell, but at least now I have some strategies to deal with it. I have used these strategies successfully in the past.

then this is much less likely to happen. This second interpretation of his experiences has a much less catastrophic feel to it, so it is much less likely that Calvin will suffer from an escalation of his difficulties. This example shows why it is important to develop a balanced appraisal of the future emergence of problems in order to reduce the risk of relapse.

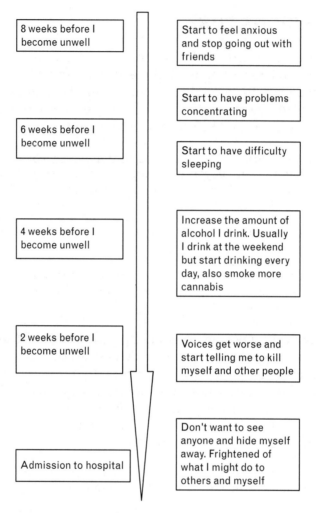

Constructing a time line is often useful because it helps us to identify those problems that indicate that relapse is a possibility, but also because it helps us to identify when to act in order to stop this from happening. For example, we can imagine that if Calvin starts to worry about his feelings of anxiety, it might be a good time for him to start using thought records again. He might use these to challenge his concerns about his experiences and to find a less catastrophic interpretation of what is happening to him. Alternatively, he could use thought records to check out other worries he is having. Additionally, at this point Calvin might be wise to consider asking his general practitioner for a specific anxiety management medication. In fact, in order to plan for emergencies, suitable interventions can be written on the time line, as shown opposite.

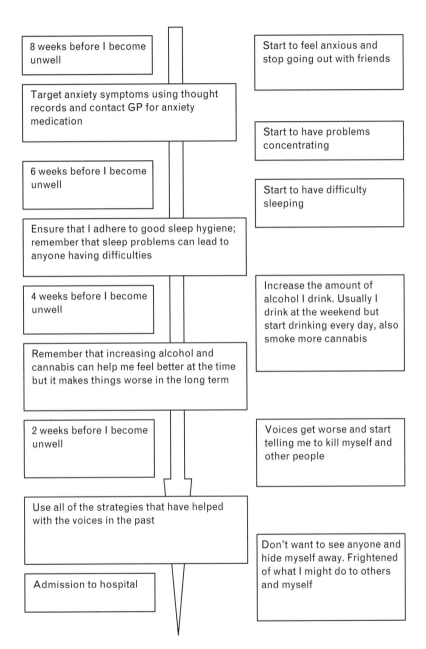

8 weeks before I become unwell	Start to feel anxious and stop going out with friends
Target anxiety symptoms using thought records and contact GP for anxiety medication	Start to have problems concentrating
6 weeks before I become unwell	Start to have difficulty sleeping
Ensure that I adhere to good sleep hygiene; remember that sleep problems can lead to anyone having difficulties	
4 weeks before I become unwell	Increase the amount of alcohol I drink. Usually I drink at the weekend but start drinking every day, also smoke more cannabis
Remember that increasing alcohol and cannabis can help me feel better at the time but it makes things worse in the long term	
2 weeks before I become unwell	Voices get worse and start telling me to kill myself and other people
Use all of the strategies that have helped with the voices in the past	
Admission to hospital	Don't want to see anyone and hide myself away. Frightened of what I might do to others and myself

In the table earlier, there are examples of some of the experiences that people may have as part of the build up to a relapse. Using the list that you generated, now fill in your own time line and consider strategies that might be useful at the different points in time (you may want to discuss this with someone you trust).

Fill in your own time line from the information you have collected

8 weeks before I become unwell

6 weeks before I become unwell

4 weeks before I become unwell

2 weeks before I become unwell

FORMULATION

Another approach to staying well involves the use of what psychologists and cognitive therapists call a *formulation*. This is a diagram that tries to explain how your problems developed and what is keeping them going. This brings together many of the factors that have been considered in earlier chapters, such as the way that you are interpreting events, your feelings and your behaviour, as well as your life experiences and the beliefs that you have formed as a result of them.

The theory on which such formulations are based [18] suggests that our life experience leads us to develop beliefs about ourselves and others, and that these, in turn, affect the way we make sense of events. If our interpretations of events are unusual or culturally unacceptable, then they are likely to be viewed as a sign of psychosis. If our responses to these events and interpretations are unhelpful, such as feeling strong negative emotions or behaving in ways that may be problematic such as safety behaviours, then vicious cycles may develop that maintain these difficulties.

CATH'S FORMULATION

As we have seen, Cath's difficulties began after she had her first child. She believed that the police were working with the local social services department to plan her prosecution and that they let themselves into her house when she goes out, and rearrange items such as ornaments and small pieces of furniture in order to remind her that they are watching her. When she went out, Cath kept her head down, looked at the pavement and counted in her head, in order to prevent police officers and social workers from reading her mind. These beliefs made her feel very scared, and she often felt tired. Cath had believed 'I am bad', 'I am worthless' and 'I am stupid' since she was very young, because she had often been told such things at home and school, and her parents had been very critical of her. Cath's therapist summarized this information in a formulation that Cath took home to decide whether it made sense. She found it helpful, and together they used it in order to think about how it could help her stay well. They decided that she should keep using the strategies she had developed to make her feel better about herself, and that she would use strategies for evaluating her thoughts and testing her beliefs if she became distressed by psychotic experiences in the future.

YOUR FORMULATION

It might be helpful for you to try to summarize the information that you have gained about your problems by developing a formulation (you

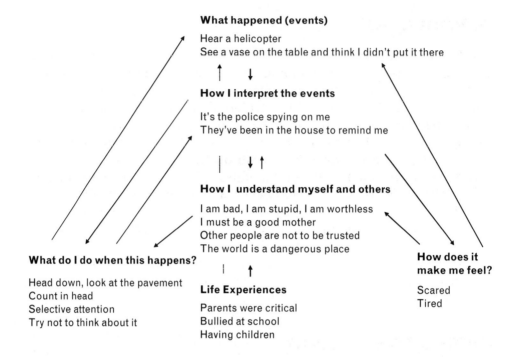

What happened (events)

Hear a helicopter
See a vase on the table and think I didn't put it there

How I interpret the events

It's the police spying on me
They've been in the house to remind me

How I understand myself and others

I am bad, I am stupid, I am worthless
I must be a good mother
Other people are not to be trusted
The world is a dangerous place

What do I do when this happens?

Head down, look at the pavement
Count in head
Selective attention
Try not to think about it

Life Experiences

Parents were critical
Bullied at school
Having children

How does it make me feel?

Scared
Tired

might want to do this with the help of your therapist). Use this framework to see if you can understand how your problems might have developed and what factors keep them going. You can write down your life experiences and how these made you see yourself, other people and the world (see Chapter 8). You can also write down the events and your distressing interpretations of them, how this makes you feel and how you behave (see Chapters 4–6). This formulation may help you to prevent future difficulties, by thinking about what strategies would be sensible to carry on using in order to stay well.

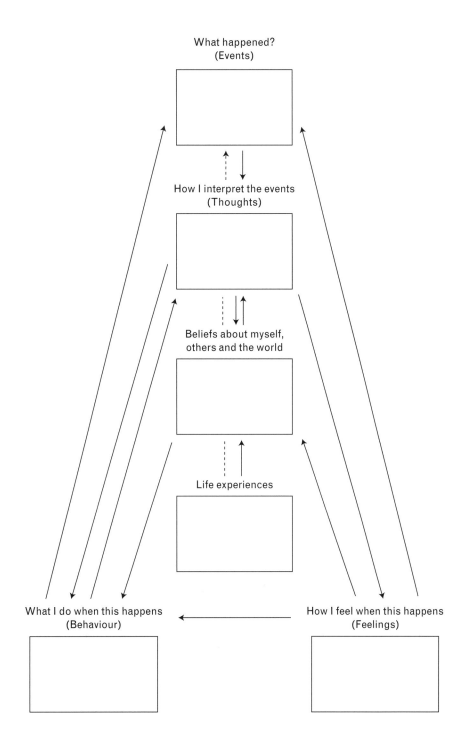

What happened?
(Events)

How I interpret the events
(Thoughts)

Beliefs about myself,
others and the world

Life experiences

What I do when this happens
(Behaviour)

How I feel when this happens
(Feelings)

10

Using medication

Calvin has always had mixed feelings about the medication that his psychiatrist and his CPN keep encouraging him to take. His first experience of the drugs – being forced down by the nurses on the psychiatric ward and then having the medication injected into his backside – was not a good start. The experience was terrifying and the drugs, if anything, made him feel worse at first. Shortly after the first injection, he had begun to feel simultaneously very agitated and extremely depressed. It had been as if sitting still was impossible but, at the same time, he was too lacking in energy to move. Over the next few days these feelings had gradually subsided, but had then been replaced with strange problems afflicting his body. He had become stiff and experienced difficulty moving. At the same time he had started to shake uncontrollably, and he had been unable to sit in a chair without his legs swinging in front of him. These experiences had only served to magnify the sense of anger and injustice that had led to his admission to hospital in the first place. At first he had wondered whether they proved that there was something wrong with his brain after all, as his psychiatrist insisted. Then, after talking to some of the other patients who were suffering from similar problems, he had realized that they were caused by the medication, and he had come to the conclusion that the doctors and nurses were trying to poison him. This suspicion was reinforced by the fact that none of the nurses would give him a straight answer when he asked them about the effects of the medication. They just told him that the medication was being given to him for his own good, that he should keep on taking it and that he had no choice over the matter in any case.

In the following years, Calvin had taken his medication intermittently. As time passed, and especially when his psychiatrist had given him some additional drugs to counter the side effects of the drugs he was being given for his psychosis, the shakes and stiffness had become less of a problem. However, he began to experience other problems, which were less obvious to other people but just as bad so far as Calvin was concerned. For example, he lost his ability to have an erection. Also, he began to feel very lethargic, unmotivated and emotionally flat.

On several occasions, Calvin had decided to stop taking his medication. As soon as he did, he started to feel more alive and happy with the world. His energy returned. Unfortunately, his voices also tended to get worse. Twice, his CPN had noticed these changes, and had persuaded him to begin taking the medication again. On each of these occasions, the implicit threat of being sent back to hospital if his symptoms worsened had been the main factor persuading Calvin to continue with the treatment.

In this chapter we will deal with one of the thorniest issues that has to be faced by someone experiencing psychosis: whether or not to take psychiatric drugs. The issue is thorny because professionals' attitudes towards drug treatment tend to be highly polarized (with most psychiatrists arguing that it is an essential component of effective treatment, but quite a few psychologists and even a few psychiatrists arguing that it can cause more harm than good) and because, despite these differences of opinion, many patients feel that they have no choice but to take drugs, whatever their effects. Our own view (which experience has told us makes us few friends in either camp) is that drug treatment is extremely helpful to some people but harmful to others. For this reason we think that it is important that all patients are helped to make a rational decision about whether to choose to try this kind of treatment. The purpose of this chapter is to provide some of the information that people with psychosis, their friends and family need for this purpose. In fact, we will only be able to touch on some of the main issues, and it's a good idea to read around widely on this topic, if at all possible (we recommend for this purpose David Healy's book *Psychiatric Drugs Explained* [31]). Unfortunately, the staff at psychiatric clinics sometimes treat patients as if they are incapable of making choices or even understanding much about their drugs. However, there is no reason why most patients – even if lacking a formal education – cannot acquire detailed knowledge of the treatment they are receiving.

A BIT OF BACKGROUND

There are many different kinds of psychiatric drugs and, often to the confusion of the people who take them, each has two or more names. For example, the drug chlorpromazine (to use its *chemical* name) is also known by its trade name Largactil in the UK, and by the name Thorazine in the USA. Fortunately, each of the drugs falls into one of four main classes, which makes the task of understanding their effects not too difficult.

Antipsychotics

The antipsychotic (sometimes called neuroleptic) drugs are almost invariably prescribed to people with psychotic experiences, and the bulk of this chapter will therefore focus on them. The first drug of this type, chlorpromazine, was discovered by a French naval surgeon, Henri Laborit, who, shortly after the end of the Second World War, was trying to find a drug that would help his patients tolerate the shock of emergency surgery. Chlorpromazine had recently been synthesized by a drug company, who sent him samples so that he could study its effects. It appeared to do nothing to help his surgical patients, but he noticed that, after they had taken it, they seemed to be very indifferent to their surroundings. With a flash of lateral thinking, Laborit wondered whether psychiatric patients might find this feeling of indifference beneficial, and persuaded some of his psychiatric colleagues to try it with their patients. When two distinguished professors of psychiatry in Paris heard of Laborit's experiments, they immediately carried out a detailed study, which revealed that the drug had apparently remarkable effects on the symptoms of manic patients. Within a few years of Laborit's discovery, chlorpromazine was being used around the world. In the light of how well the drug was selling, other drug companies rushed to develop their own versions of chlorpromazine, mainly by manufacturing compounds that were chemically similar and testing them on patients. At this stage, no one had a clue how chlorpromazine and the rapidly expanding group of similar drugs worked. However, in the late 1950s it was discovered that the brain used a chemical called dopamine to transmit messages between different nerve cells, and, shortly afterwards, that all of the successful antipsychotics interfered with this process. This led to the widespread acceptance of a theory that is debated to this day – that psychotic symptoms are caused by some kind of abnormality in the brain cells that use dopamine.

Interestingly, professionals' views about the nature and effects of antipsychotics have shifted over the 50 years since they were developed. The indifference that was seen as their main beneficial effect by the early French researchers soon became viewed as a side effect. The same early researchers recognized that antipsychotics produced numerous other side effects that were distressing to patients, most notably Parkinsonism (so-called because they mimic the brain disease Parkinson's syndrome, which causes patients to shake violently and to 'freeze' so that their bodies will not respond to decisions to move) and tardive dyskinesia (uncontrollable movements of the mouth and tongue, a disorder that was often permanent, even after drug treatment had discontinued). However, they believed that these side effects were necessary for the drugs to have their antipsychotic effect, and that patients should be encouraged to take them nonetheless. When, in the 1970s, a group of German researchers claimed to have found an antipsychotic called clozapine that did not produce these effects, most psychiatrists doubted that this was possible. When early experiments with the drug in Finland resulted in a number of fatalities, it was also discovered that clozapine caused a life-threatening blood-disease, agranularcytosis, in about one in a hundred patients.

Clozapine would have been added to a long list of failed medical experiments had some American researchers not realized that it might nonetheless be useful as a treatment for patients suffering from severe Parkinsonism and tardive dyskinesia. They found that they could detect agranularcytosis early enough to prevent it becoming fatal if they tested patients' blood at regular intervals. (This is why, if you are asked to take clozapine, you will be given a blood test every one or two weeks.) In a series of experiments they found that clozapine was sometimes an effective treatment for patients who failed to respond to any other kind of medication.

Once again, drug companies have rushed to find other compounds with similar effects. Over the last few years a number of *atypical antipsychotics* have been put on the market, and it is possible that you will be asked to take one. Many psychiatrists believe that these drugs are 'kinder' or 'better tolerated' (that is, they have fewer side effects) than the older typical antipsychotics, and some even believe that they are more effective (that is, that they are more likely to have a beneficial effect on hallucinations and delusions (but see more about this issue below)).

Most antipsychotic drugs are taken as tablets. However, some can be given as *depot* medications, which means that they are injected into a muscle (in the backside) every 2–4 weeks. Once in the body, they are slowly released over the period before the next injection is given. From the patient's point of view, the only real advantage of a depot injection is that it may be more convenient – there is no need to remember to take pills every day. From the point of view of the doctor, however, the main advantage is usually that the patient finds it much more difficult to stop taking the medication (of course, in the event of a severe adverse reaction to the drug, this can be a medical problem rather than a benefit). Therefore, psychiatrists often try to persuade patients to accept depot medications when they suspect that the patient may be reluctant to take drugs. In our view, this approach is rarely satisfactory for either the patient or the doctor. After all, patients can avoid depot medications simply by refusing to turn up to their regular clinic appointments.

The following table (adapted from the similar table in David Healy's book [31]) lists some of the most frequently prescribed antipsychotic drugs, giving their chemical names and their trade names.

Drug name	UK trade name	US trade name
Typical antipsychotics		
Chlorpromazine	Largactil	Thorazine
Flupenthixol	Fluanxol/Depixol	n/a
Zuclopenthixol	Clopixol	n/a
Perphenazine	Fentazin	Trilafon
Trifluoperazine	Stelazine	Stelazine
Pericyazine	Neulactil	Neulactil
Promazine	Sparine	n/a
Loxapine	Loxitan/Loxapac	Loxitane
Sulpiride	Sulpitil/Dolmatil/Sulparex	n/a
Haloperidol	Serenace/Haldol/Dozic	Haldol
Tetrabenazine	Xenazine	
Molindone	n/a	Moban/Lidone
Atypical antipsychotics		
Clozapine	Clozaril	Clozaril
Risperidone	Risperdal	Risperdal
Olanzapine	Zyprexa	Zyprexa
Quetiapine	Seroquel	Seroquel
Ziprasidone	n/a	Geodon
Amisulpride	Solian	n/a
Aripiprazole	Abilify	Abilify
Zotepine	Zoleptil	n/a

Mood stabilizers

The second major class of psychiatric drugs are the mood stabilizers. The first drug of this type, lithium carbonate, was discovered in the 1950s by an Australian physician, Brian Cade, who, by a series of accidental steps, discovered that this substance had a highly calming effect on agitated patients if they were injected with it. Unfortunately, psychiatrists and drug companies were slow to follow Cade's lead, probably because he was not a widely respected researcher, but also because the drug companies could see no way of making major profits from a naturally occurring compound that cannot be patented. For these reasons, lithium carbonate only became widely available in the 1970s. Since that time it has been widely used to treat patients who have severe mood swings. (As we saw in Chapter 1, patients with this problem are often diagnosed as suffering from *manic depression* or *bipolar disorder*. However, this drug can be used in the treatment of any psychiatric patient who suffers from severe changes in mood.) Possible side effects include tremor, thirst and increased frequency of urination, kidney problems, weight gain, diar rhoea, skin rashes or irritations, hair loss, tiredness, tension and restless-ness, concentration problems and headache. Lithium can be toxic at high concentrations in the blood, and ineffective if the concentration is too low. Unfortunately, it can be difficult to predict blood levels from the dose taken, so patients receiving this kind of treatment usually need to have regular blood tests.

In recent years, doctors have begun to look for more effective mood stabilizers, and it has been discovered that some anticonvulsant drugs usually used in the treatment of epilepsy can have this effect. Examples that are now sometimes prescribed to patients include carbamazepine, valproate and lamotrigine.

Antidepressants

Antidepressants, as the name suggests, are often used in the treatment of depression. The earliest drugs of this kind, introduced in the early 1960s, were known as tricyclics because of their chemical structure. Examples included amitripyline (Tryptizol or Lentizol in the UK, Elavil or Endep in the USA), imipramine (Tofranil in both the UK and the USA), and clomipramine (Anafranil in the UK and the USA) and these medications are still in use today. However, patients have often found that these drugs produce side effects such as sedation, difficulty sleeping, dry mouth, low blood pressure causing a risk of fainting, palpitations, problems passing water, sweating, tremor, blurred vision and nausea. In the late 1970s, therefore, a new class of antidepressant was introduced, known as the selective serotonin re-uptake inhibitors (SSRIs) because of their effect on parts of the brain that use the chemical serotonin (which is thought to have an important role in controlling mood). The most famous SSRI was fluoxetine (Prozac in the UK and the USA), which was hyped to such a degree that several novels made reference to it in their titles. Many similar drugs have been manufactured since, for example paroxetine (Seroxat in the UK, Paxil in the USA) and sertraline (Lustral in the UK, Effexor in the USA).

In fact, the latest evidence suggests that these new drugs are no more effective than the older antidepressant medications, although they may be less unpleasant to take (they have fewer and less troubling side effects). A serious problem with some of the new drugs is that, in a very small proportion of patients, they may cause severe agitation when first taken. There has even been a suggestion that – extremely rarely – patients become so agitated that they attack other people or feel prompted to commit suicide. This issue is highly controversial and most drug companies either deny that these effects occur, or that they occur so rarely that the risk to individual patients is too small to worry about. Certainly, many people take this kind of medication without experiencing this kind of side effect.

Anxiolytics

The final class of drugs that will be briefly mentioned here is the anxiolytics. The most common of these are known as benzodiazepines, and include diazepam (Valium in the UK and the USA), lorazepam (Ativan in the UK and the USA) and alprazolam (Xanax in the UK and the USA). In the early 1970s these drugs were thought to be almost miracle treatments for people suffering from persistent emotional problems, and were believed to be incapable of causing harmful side effects. They were widely prescribed by family doctors to people suffering from feelings of anxiety and depression.

In fact, it soon became apparent that the benzodiazepines had a serious drawback, in that withdrawal from the medication often led to feelings of anxiety and agitation. As it was often precisely these symptoms that led doctors to prescribe these kinds of drugs in the first place, patients who felt that they had improved enough to stop taking their medication often felt that their problems were returning, began taking their medication again, and soon found themselves trapped in a cycle of dependence. Eventually, it became necessary to establish specialist clinics to help patients who wished to live without benzodiazepines.

None of this is to say that these kinds of drugs cannot be useful under some circumstances. Because they have few side effects in the short term (over a few weeks), they can be used to reduce anxiety in a crisis. Recently, evidence has also emerged to show that these drugs can be as effective (and much kinder in terms of side effects) than high-dose antipsychotic drugs (the more conventional alternative) for treating the high levels of distress and agitation experienced by patients during the early stages of an acute psychotic episode.

As we have already said, if you suffer from psychotic experiences you are likely to be encouraged to take an antipsychotic drug. However, your doctor may also try to prescribe you a mood stabilizer, or an antidepressant, or a benzodiazapine, or any combination of these. (It is not unusual to find that patients are taking all four main types of drugs – this often means that the doctor feels 'stuck'.) However, because antipsychotics are the main drug treatment used with psychotic patients, the rest of our discussion will focus on these.

ANTIPSYCHOTIC DRUGS: THE FACTS

If you are to make an informed choice about your drug treatment, you will need to understand the advantages and disadvantages of the medication your doctor has prescribed for you. Because each drug has a tendency to produce a unique combination of effects and side effects, and because different people tend to experience these effects and side effects to different degrees, it is a good idea to learn as much as possible about the particular medication you have been prescribed. A little later we will consider how you might do this. Before we do this, however, we will consider some general information about antipsychotics.

The benefits of antipsychotic drugs

There is no doubt that antipsychotic drugs have beneficial effects for some patients. Many experiments have convincingly demonstrated that the majority of patients receiving antipsychotic drugs experience some relief from their difficulties, such as hearing voices or distressing unusual beliefs (hallucinations and delusions). Although precise numbers are difficult to estimate, probably about 70% of patients benefit in this way (which, of course, means that about 30% of patients do not benefit).

However, this good news has to be qualified by two important considerations. First, in order to obtain maximum benefit from antipsychotic drugs, it may be necessary to keep on taking them, even after making a complete recovery from psychotic symptoms. In a number of experiments this type of treatment – known as prophylactic therapy – has been compared with the obvious alternative, intermittent therapy, in which the patient only takes medication when feeling stressed or unwell. In general, it has been found that patients who have been prescribed prophylactic therapy are less likely to relapse (suffer an increase in symptoms leading to a hospital admission) than patients treated intermittently (although one recent study found that intermittent therapy may be just as effective for patients experiencing their first episode of psychosis). If you are considering drug treatment this finding has an important implication – to get maximum benefit you may have to keep taking the drugs for a number of years. Of course it is natural to ask 'How many years?', but unfortunately the existing research provides no indication of when it may be safe to discontinue taking antipsychotics. In our experience, most psychiatrists are willing to consider slowly reducing the dose of antipsychotics after a couple of years have passed since the last episode.

Side effects of antipsychotic drugs

The second important qualification about the effects of antipsychotics is that they have numerous side effects, some of which can be distressing or threatening to long-term health. In describing these side effects it is not our intention to frighten you. In times gone past, psychiatrists were sometimes reluctant to talk to patients about common antipsychotic side effects for this reason, but we think that you need to be fully informed about them if you are to make a rational decision about whether or not to try this type of treatment. Of course, not everyone who takes antipsychotic drugs experiences all of these side effects, and many patients find that the side effects that they do experience are tolerable compared to the distress associated with hallucinations and delusions.

The most common antipsychotic side effects are shown in the table below. The table shows side effects for the typical antipsychotics and the atypicals. It is important to remember that not everyone will experience these side effects to the same degree. It is also important to remember that different people experiencing the same side effect may be bothered by it to different degrees. One person may feel that a side effect is well worth tolerating because of the benefits that a drug brings in reducing distress. Another patient taking the same drug may feel that the side effect is so bothersome that he or she would rather go without the drug, despite its beneficial effects.

It is important to understand the likely side effects of the particular medication you are taking. Sometimes doctors and nurses are afraid to tell their patients about side effects because they fear that this will put the patients off the medication. However, patients are usually much more willing to put up with side effects if warned of them in advance. Conversely, it can be frightening and disorientating to experience a symptom and not know whether it is caused by illness or treatment.

Side effect	Description/comments
Extrapyramidal effects	These effects usually occur only following treatment with typical antipsychotics. With the exception of tardive dyskinesia, they usually disappear when medication is discontinued.
Stiffness and lack of movement	Slowing down of normal movements; in extremis, may lead to the feeling of being straitjacketed. Can lead to clumsiness.
Dyskinesias	Abnormal movements, most often affecting the arms and hands, varying from a fine tremor to a repetitive rotation of the wrist known as a 'pill rolling' movement. If the legs are affected it may be difficult to sit still.
Dystonias	Abrupt muscular spasms, which usually last less than an hour. If the eyes are affected, an oculogyric crisis may occur in which the eyeballs roll into the top of the head. If the facial muscles are affected, swallowing may be difficult.
Akathisia	An unpleasant subjective sensation of severe restlessness and agitation, often accompanied by depression, most often experienced during the first few days of treatment.
Tardive dyskinesia	Unsightly abnormal movements of the mouth and tongue. Affecting 5–20% of patients taking antipsychotics, this side effect may persist months or years after medication is discontinued.
Other common effects	
Loss of motivation	Patients taking antipsychotics may feel a loss of drive and emotional blunting, leading to reduced success in relationships and work.
Weight gain	Weight gain is a serious side effect of many antipsychotics, but especially clozapine and olanzapine, with increases of 20 kg not being unusual. The causes are unknown but may include increased appetite and reduced activity. Weight gain may have serious long-term implications for health.
Diabetes	Diabetes can occur with all antipsychotics, but is a problem particularly associated with the long-term use of olanzapine and clozapine. This side effect seems to be independent of weight gain (which, on its own, can increase the risk of diabetes).
Sexual dysfunction	Sexual dysfunction, including the inability to maintain an erection in the case of males, is a common side effect of most antipsychotics.
Hormonal changes	With the exception of clozapine and quetiapine, antipsychotics increase production of the hormone prolactin, leading to lactation (production of breast milk), swelling of breasts (which can occasionally occur in men) and, in women, disruption of the menstrual cycle.

Side effect	Description/comments
Skin problems	Rashes are common. In the case of chlorpromazine, extreme sun sensitivity may occur, requiring sun cream even on mild days in order to prevent burning.
Sedation	This may be especially problematic at high doses.
Thirst	Excessive need to drink water may be experienced.
Epilepsy	Fitting may occur in vulnerable individuals, especially after treatment with atypical antipsychotics (rare).
Rare, life-threatening effects	
Neuroleptic malignant sydrome	A condition that begins with fever and stiffness, rather like flu; can be fatal unless antipsychotic treatment is not discontinued.
Cardiac problems	Some antipsychotics carry a risk of cardiac arrhythmias (irregular beating of the heart).
Agranulocytosis	Proliferation of the white blood cells, which is most associated with clozapine (affecting approx 1% of patients treated for two years). Can be fatal unless drug treatment is discontinued. For this reason, regular blood monitoring will be required if you take this drug.

SOME MYTHS ABOUT ANTIPSYCHOTIC TREATMENT

We have so far considered the major benefits and side effects of anti-psychotic drugs. However, before we go on to discuss how you can use this information to decide whether antipsychotic therapy might be help-ful to you, we must address a few important myths about this kind of treatment, myths that are shared by many professionals and patients alike.

Myth 1: Antipsychotics are anti-schizophrenia drugs

Most textbooks of psychiatry assume that antipsychotic drugs are anti-schizophrenia drugs. However, schizophrenia is not the only diagnosis given to people with psychotic symptoms (as we saw in Chapter 2, some patients are diagnosed as suffering from bipolar disorder, schizoaffective disorder or delusional disorder, depending on the exact combination of symptoms they experience). In fact, there is no evidence that people with any one of these diagnoses benefit from the drugs more than people with any other (after all, the first successful trial of chlorpromazine was carried out with manic patients). However, there is evidence that hallucinations and delusions are more likely to respond to antipsychotic medication than other symptoms. Implication – it might make sense to consider this kind of medication if you suffer from these symptoms, but otherwise you might want to think twice.

Myth 2: All patients with psychotic symptoms benefit from antipsychotic drugs

Conversely, whereas some people with diagnoses other than schizo-phrenia benefit from antipsychotics, some people with the diagnosis don't. Probably about a quarter of patients with voices or abnormal beliefs fail to benefit from antipsychotic medication at all. Nobody really knows why this is the case, or how to predict who will benefit and who will not. Implication – antipsychotic drugs should be tried on a 'suck-it-and-see' basis (you need to find out for yourself whether these drugs benefit you).

Myth 3: The new atypical antipsychotics are more effective (better at reducing symptoms) than the old typical antipsychotics

With the possible exception of clozapine (which some experts believe helps a proportion of patients who fail to respond to other drugs), there is no evidence that one antipsychotic is more effective than any other. The main advantage of the atypicals is that they do not cause Parkinsonian side effects. For this reason, they may be less unpleasant to take than the older type of medication. However, it is important to remember that only the person who is taking the medication can decide which side effects are most troublesome. Some of the newer drugs, for example olanzapine, cause problems such as weight gain, diabetes and sexual dysfunction that, although less obvious to others, may be just as bothersome as Parkinsonian side effects such as tremor and stiffness.

Myth 4: If you fail to benefit from one antipsychotic, another may work better

More importantly, a patient who fails to benefit from an antipsychotic is unlikely to respond to any other, again with the possible exception of clozapine. We have quite often come across patients who have been encouraged to try an apparently endless succession of antipsychotics over a period of years in the hope that an effective one will eventually be found by a process of trial and error, but the scientific literature shows that this strategy has no rational basis. Implication – if you have tried more than three different antipsychotics and then clozapine without any beneficial effect, you should almost certainly give up on this kind of treatment.

Myth 5: High doses of antipsychotics are sometimes necessary

Earlier in this chapter, we saw that the pioneers of antipsychotic therapy believed that Parkinsonian side effects – and hence high doses of drugs – were required to get an antipsychotic effect. Incredibly, it was not until the early 1990s that this idea was tested in the first experiments that looked at the relationship between drug dose and antipsychotic treatment response. The results of these experiments were a surprise to many psychiatrists, as they showed that low doses of antipsychotics worked at least as well as high doses. As low dose treatment is likely to cause fewer side effects, this type of treatment is almost always preferable to high dose treatment.

Myth 6: Sometimes it is necessary to take more than one antipsychotic drug

Doctors sometimes prescribe more than one antipsychotic drug to a patient, usually when a patient has not benefited from a single anti-psychotic. There is no evidence that combining antipsychotics in this way is beneficial, and experts in drug treatment usually advise against it. The practice is particularly irrational when, as sometimes happens, a doctor prescribes a typical antipsychotic and an atypical antipsychotic at the same time. The main advantage of an atypical antipsychotic is that it does not cause the Parkinsonian side effects associated with the typical anti-psychotics; clearly this advantage will be lost if a typical antipsychotic is given at the same time.

UNDERSTANDING THE EFFECTS OF YOUR MEDICATION: GETTING INFORMATION

Calvin decided that he needed to know more about the medication he was receiving. In the past, his doctors and nurses had been reluctant to talk to him about the effects and side effects of his treatment, but he felt confident that Dr Skinner, his new psychiatrist, would be more helpful.

When asked, Dr Skinner quickly ran through some basic information about the effects and side effects of antipsychotics. However, he only had about 15 minutes, and he acknowledged that this would not be enough to provide Calvin with all the information he needed. 'I wish I had some more time', Dr Skinner said, 'but unfortunately there are other patients who are waiting to see me. We can arrange to meet another time, if you'd like, but let me tell you about some other places you can get information from.' Dr Skinner wrote down the details of David Healy's book, *Psychiatric Drugs Explained* on a piece of paper, and suggested that Calvin got hold of a copy from the library.

Dr Skinner also suggested that Calvin read the information sheet provided inside Calvin's medication packet. Calvin had noticed this sheet every time he got a new packet of medication. However, he had never taken the trouble to read it. When he got home that afternoon, Calvin found the sheet and looked at it carefully. He was surprised to discover that it was quite easy to read. There was quite a lot of information, so Calvin decided to read it several times over. Indeed, over the following few days, he picked up the sheet and studied it several times.

Finally, Dr Skinner told Calvin that he would make an appointment for him to see a psychiatric pharmacist. 'The pharmacist is the real expert on drugs', Dr Skinner explained. 'In fact, she knows more about the effects of medication than I do. I'll ask her to see you specially, so that she can explain what the medication does in detail.'

If you are taking medication there are many places where you can find out about the effects and side effects of drugs. Even if your doctor is too busy to spend much time discussing your medication with you, like Calvin you can read the information sheet that is given with your drugs (drug companies are legally required to provide these), you can ask other mental health professionals for help (it is worth asking to speak to a psychiatric pharmacist, but remember, if one is not available in your area, other professionals such as CPNs may be able to provide the information you need) and you can consult books such as David Healy's *Psychiatric Drugs*

Explained [31]. You can also look up your medication on the Internet – but, be warned, not all the information on the Internet is accurate.

WORKING OUT WHETHER YOUR DRUGS ARE HELPING YOU

If offered medication, or if you have been taking medication for some time but are worried about whether it is really working for you, you will need to carry out your own personal cost–benefit analysis of its effects. The aim of this exercise is to find out for yourself what the benefits of the medication are, but also whether there are any harmful or distressing side effects that outweigh these benefits. A good psychiatrist or psychiatric nurse will help you in this process, by providing you with advice and information.

If you are taking antipsychotic drugs for the first time

It is usually assumed that antipsychotic drugs take about four weeks to work, although benefits are sometimes more immediate. During this time, some unpleasant side effects (for example, feelings of restlessness and agitation) tend to reduce in severity, whereas others (for example, feelings of lethargy and loss of motivation) may increase. Unfortunately, some people taking this kind of treatment make snap judgements about its effectiveness on the basis of a few days, or even a few hours, of treatment. Realistically, there is little alternative to sticking with the medication for 4–6 weeks before forming an opinion about its advantages and dis-advantages. During this period, it makes sense to:

- Obtain as much information about the medication as possible.
- Keep a diary of any positive and negative effects you might experience. Unpleasant side effects tend to be easier to notice than positive effects. For example, you may notice that you are putting on weight but the gradual reduction in fear of other people that you might experience may be more difficult to spot. At the end of four weeks, it will make sense to try to think back to how you were feeling when first given medication. Have things improved for you over this period? Are you feeling less distressed? Are you still hearing voices? Are you still scared of other people to the same extent?
- Before going to talk to your doctor, prepare what you are going to say. Write down any questions you want to ask. If you are experiencing unpleasant side effects, work out (perhaps with the help of a friend) how to tell the doctor

about them. If you are worried about your dose of medication, do not be afraid to discuss this. You might also want to consider taking someone you trust along with you.

If you have been taking antipsychotic drugs for some time

Many patients take medication for long periods of time without realizing its protective effect (that is, its tendency to prevent relapse), only to discover this after suddenly discontinuing treatment against medical advice and becoming suddenly distressed and confused. Conversely, some patients end up taking medication unnecessarily for many years because no one – patient, doctor or nurse – thought to review whether the medication was being helpful. Whatever your situation, it makes sense to review your medical treatment from time to time.

⊙ Write a history of your medical treatment in note form. This can be drawn on a large piece of paper as a time-line, on which each year is represented by a few inches of line, against which you can mark critical incidents and achievements such as admissions to hospital, completing educational courses, moving house, making new friends etc. Try to work out when you first began taking psychiatric drugs, and when the medication has been changed. Also, make a note of any occasions on which you discontinued medication for whatever reason. (Perhaps there was a period a few years ago when you decided that you did not need to take your medication.) Now look at your notes and see whether there is any relationship between the medication you were taking and what happened to you. Did you feel worse when taking a particular type of medication? Did you stop medication without any negative consequences, or have there been times when you decided to stop and became ill soon afterwards? If stopping medication in the past has made things worse, what were the consequences? Was your ability to work, or to get on with your friends, affected?

⊙ Find out as much as possible about the medication you are currently taking. Write down a list of known side effects (for example, by reading the leaflet that comes with the medication). Go through the list and note whether you are currently experiencing any of the side effects on the list. Also, note how bothered you are by each side effect (for example, by using a simple numerical scale on which 0 = not bothered at all and 10 = extremely distressed by the side effect).

⊙ Write down a list of pros and cons for your medical treatment. What are the advantages of continuing to take it? What are the disadvantages?

⊙ Consider whether your medication needs adjusting. For example, if you are experiencing distressing side effects, is it worth asking your doctor to reduce the dose? If the drugs do not seem to be benefiting you very much, does it make sense to ask the doctor to increase the dose or to switch you to an alternative drug? What about asking your doctor about alternative (non-drug) treatments such as psychological therapies?

⊙ Before talking to your doctor, prepare what you are going to say. Write down any questions you want to ask. If you are experiencing unpleasant side effects, work out (perhaps with the help of a friend) how to tell the doctor about them. If you are worried about your dose of medication, do not be afraid to discuss this.

⊙ If you have been on medication for several years, and if you have been well for a long time, do not be afraid to ask your doctor to withdraw the treatment. Just as when taking medication for the first time, withdrawing from drug treatment must be done on a 'suck-it-and-see' basis, monitoring any effects as they happen (see below). Remember, antipsychotic drugs must be withdrawn very gradually (over a period of months) to minimize the risk of a relapse.

STICKING TO YOUR DRUG TREATMENT

No drug treatment can be effective unless the drugs are taken. Unfortunately, most people find taking medication over a long period of time extremely difficult. It is all too easy to forget to take your drugs. This is just as true for medical patients as for psychiatric patients – many patients prescribed an antibiotic will stop taking their medication as soon as they feel better, and will not continue to take their drugs until the course is finished as recommended by doctors.

In order to take medication effectively, you are going to need to develop a routine that allows your drugs to fit into your life. The exact routine you choose will depend on the type of medication you take, for example on how many tablets you need to take each day. Here are a few tips:

⊙ A lot of drugs, especially drugs that are taken once a day, come in blister packs, with each day's medication labelled (for example, each blister may be labelled with a day of the week). This is supposed to help you notice if you accidentally miss your medication (for example, on looking at the packet on Thursday you may notice that Wednesday's medication is still there).

⊙ Never vary your medication against medical advice. Sometimes people who are taking tablets decide to either increase their medication or decrease it without consulting their doctor. For example, we know of one patient who increased his medication after a night out drinking (because he thought that the drink might dilute it) and another who decreased it in the same circumstances (because she thought that medication and drink did not mix). Varying medication in this way is usually a bad idea, unless the doctor has specifically suggested doing so.

◉ Try to time your medication so that you take it at the same time every day, preferably when you regularly do something else. For example, if you have to take a tablet first thing in the morning, always take it just after brushing your teeth or with your first cup of coffee. In this way, you will develop automatic habits for taking tablets, and you will easily remember to take them.

◉ If you have a lot of difficulty remembering to take your medication, you could try leaving yourself cues to remind you. For example, you could tape a notice saying 'Have you taken your drugs yet?' next to the bathroom mirror. It will also help to keep the medication is a sensible place. For example, if you decide to take your morning tablet with your first cup of coffee of the day, you could keep your medication next to the coffee jar.

◉ If you really are having a lot of difficulty, you could try asking someone who lives with you to remind you.

◉ In the best of all possible worlds we would all remember to take any medication we have been prescribed as instructed, but it is easy to make mistakes. Get some specific advice about what to do if you miss one of your tablets. In most cases, it is okay to take a tablet up to a couple of hours late but, after that time, it is best to wait until the next tablet is due. Most information leaflets that come in medication packets give advice about this.

Remember, you will not be able to find out if your medication is effective for you unless you take it regularly. It is important to accept that this is difficult, and not to punish yourself when you make mistakes. If you are worried about relying on drugs, or about the stigma of taking drugs regularly, it may also help to remember that many people – and not just people who are receiving psychiatric treatment – are in this situation. There are many physical conditions that require continuous drug-taking, sometimes for decades (such as for high blood pressure).

After several weeks, Calvin had his appointment with the psychiatric pharmacist. They met at the hospital where the pharmacist worked. She spent more than half an hour with him. She began by looking at his medication packets, which he had brought with him, and writing down what he had been prescribed. Then she carefully explained what each of the drugs did, asking Calvin questions to make sure that he understood her explanations.

Calvin and the pharmacist discussed how he could remember to take his medication every day. He needed to take one tablet in the morning and another in the early evening. As Calvin was quite fastidious about cleaning his teeth, he and the pharmacist decided that the best thing to do with the morning tablet was to take it immediately afterwards. It was a bit more difficult to decide what to do with the evening tablet, as Calvin did not have a regular time for taking his evening meal. He decided to try setting the alarm on his watch for 6 pm.

Over the next week, Calvin always remembered his morning tablet, but forgot his evening tablet on three occasions. It seemed that his watch alarm was not loud enough. Also, once when he did notice his alarm going off, he was out of the house and did not have his medication with him. In the end, Calvin decided to take the tablet with his evening meal, but to try to have his meal at a more regular time. As an added help, he taped a reminder notice next to his bed, in order to prompt him to inspect his tablet packet before going to sleep to check whether he had taken the medication earlier. This was not an ideal solution, but it was an improvement. Over the following week, he twice forgot to take his tablet with his meal, but was reminded at bedtime, and took the medication then.

DECIDING TO GIVE UP DRUGS

Sometimes people receiving drug treatment for psychotic problems decide not to continue with it. Usually, doctors interpret this decision as evidence that the person concerned 'lacks insight' – that is, that they are too ill to realize that the treatment is beneficial. Sometimes, this leads the doctor to try to coerce the patient to change his or her mind. In many countries, doctors can take legal steps to compel patients to continue with their treatment. (In the UK, for example, a patient judged to present a risk to him or herself or other people can be 'sectioned', a legal manoeuvre that allows the doctor to detain him or her in hospital.)

In fact, research shows that, more commonly, people decide to give up on their drugs because they do not seem to be helping (which, as we have seen, is probably true in the case of about 25% of patients taking anti-psychotics), or because the side effects are too severe to tolerate (also true of a lot of patients). The problem, therefore, for many patients wanting to try life without medication for entirely rational reasons, is that these reasons are often doubted or disrespected by their clinicians. We should emphasize that this is not invariably the case, but it undoubtedly happens very often.

In principle, people who are voluntarily receiving psychiatric treatment (that is, those who are not on a 'section') can refuse to take the treatment. In practice, refusing outright may require a lot of courage and strength, as doctors and nurses are likely to make serious efforts to bring about a change of mind. If this is the course you choose to follow, then:

⊙ It is best to base your decision on a careful cost–benefit analysis of the advantages and disadvantages of medication, as discussed earlier.
⊙ It is best to discuss your plan with your doctor, even if you think that he or she may not be sympathetic to your decision (you could show them your cost–benefit analysis). With the help of your doctor, you should be able to plan a gradual reduction in your medication over a period of months.

Monitor your progress as the medication is reduced. Some people taking antipsychotics find that they can reduce their medication considerably, but cannot cope without some antipsychotic treatment. Even if you cannot give up antipsychotics completely, you may be able to find your optimum dose by noticing, as your dose is reduced, when feelings of anxiety and depression or other symptoms begin to return. When this happens, it is sometimes helpful to increase the dose very slightly.

⊙ It is wise not to try reducing your drugs if you are experiencing a lot of stress in your life. If you experience an unexpected stress during the course of reducing your medication, consider postponing any further reduction.

CHAPTER 11

Recovery

The possibility of recovery from psychosis is often neglected by services, as mental health professionals often have a pessimistic view of the outcomes of psychosis, which is not consistent with the scientific evidence (see Chapter 3). In this chapter we will discuss how recovery can be seen as a process or a lived experience involving the rebuilding of lives. Research suggests that recovery means different things to different people [32]. It is a gradual and uneven process without a definitive end point, and typically happens in stages involving unpredictable turning points and milestones. This research suggests that important areas for recovery include rebuilding self (understanding and empowering yourself), rebuilding life (improving relationships and active participation in life) and hope for a better future; cognitive therapy should be able to help you address each of these areas, but there are also many other ways of doing so.

CALVIN'S JOURNEY OF RECOVERY

By using the strategies that he learnt through cognitive therapy, and by testing out his fears about his voices, Calvin has become much more at ease. The therapy helped Calvin to better understand himself and to view himself as normal rather than mad, which was very important for his self-esteem. The formulation that he developed with his therapist provided a way of understanding himself and his unusual experiences, and of making sense of them in relation to his history of abuse. This helped him to reconcile his past to some extent, and provided him with some hope for the future. However, he still has some difficulties. For example, he continues to be upset by the stigma, prejudice and discrimination that he experiences because of his mental health problems.

The work that Calvin had carried out in relation to his self-esteem, gathering evidence for a more positive view of himself and recording success experiences (for example, his success at persuading his psychiatrist to lower his medication) has contributed to his recovery process. He has a good relationship with his current care coordinator, who he likes and trusts. He also has a circle of friends from the local pub and from a Hearing Voices Network group, and contact with these people has been very important to rebuilding his social life.

Calvin joined the hearing voices group in order to meet people who had had similar experiences. The group allowed him to share stories about the difficulty of coping with unpleasant voices, which he found useful. He was also able to share stories about good and bad experiences with the psychiatric system. The opportunity to express his frustration and annoyance with the mental health system's shortcomings, and about the medical model approach, in particular, was very important to Calvin. It was wonderful to have his views taken seriously and agreed with.

He thinks that it is important to have a sense of purpose in his life. He does some voluntary work with the hearing voices group and at a local cafe, which is run by service users and ex-service users. Doing this work makes him feel that he is making a useful contribution to society. He is optimistic about the possibility of a positive change in society's attitudes towards people with mental health problems, and is working with the hearing voices group to bring this change about. He is also able to reflect on how he has changed positively as a result of his experiences. He has become more able to empathize with other people's problems and is better able to understand the difficulties that are faced by people when they are very stressed and upset. He is acutely aware of the impact that child abuse can have on people, and wants to do something about this, either by making other people more aware of the effects that abuse can have or by finding ways of preventing abuse in the future. He regularly gives a small amount of money to a charity devoted to protecting children who have been abused. Calvin also hopes for changes in mental health services, and plans to do voluntary work visiting young men of African and Caribbean origin who are admitted to psychiatric hospital, in order to try to inspire hope in them.

CATH'S JOURNEY OF RECOVERY

Cognitive behaviour therapy has helped Cath to understand her difficulties and to learn strategies that can help her to feel less threatened and scared of persecution. She has also learnt to recognize the role that stress has to play in the worsening of her unusual ideas. She is aware of the benefits that medication can have for her, but also of the side effects (for example, weight gain) that upset her and present challenges to her self-esteem. She has decided on a strategy of varying her medication herself, taking it regularly when she is feeling stressed or having lots of demands made of her time, but gradually reducing her dose when she is feeling well. This seems to work, and makes her feel that she is taking responsibility for her treatment, which increases her self-esteem.

Friends and family seem particularly important for Cath's process of recovery. Over time, she has had more contact with her children, and now cooks Sunday dinner for them every week, which she enjoys. This also makes her feel like a good mother, and therefore good about herself. She tries to keep busy. She attends aerobics lessons twice a week, and goes swimming, which makes her feel healthy and also helps her to fight against the weight gain that is a consequence of her medication. She likes knitting, and makes lots of jumpers and socks for her children (who experience this as a mixed blessing). In order to keep busy and have a valued and meaningful role in life, she is also doing voluntary work in a charity shop one day a week, and recently felt sufficiently confident to successfully apply for a paid, part-time job in a bakery. She hopes that this will provide a further source of self-esteem, and help her to make new friends. All of these steps have made Cath feel that her life is worthwhile.

Now when she feels like a psychiatric patient, she reminds herself that she has successfully dealt with her mental health problems, is not totally dependent on medication, and is not alone in feeling stressed on occasion.

YOUR RECOVERY JOURNEY

We have seen that both Calvin and Cath still have some persisting problems, but that they are both well on the way to recovery. As we mentioned earlier, this process is different for everyone, and it is likely to involve setbacks as well as successes (Martina and Liz, our service user colleagues, compare it to a game of snakes and ladders).

Strategies for staying well can include making use of the techniques that you have learned in this book, as well as the formulation you developed in Chapter 9, in order to understand future problems if they occur. They might also include talking to friends and family, eating well, working and volunteering, hobbies and physical exercise. It might be useful for you to write down what you could do in some of these areas in order to help promote your own recovery, perhaps with the help of a therapist, care coordinator, friend or relative.

Please take some time to think about each of the areas identified as being important to recovery, and write down any ideas that you can think of that might help you to improve your quality of life, to remember some of the things that you have learnt about yourself, or to improve the way you feel about yourself. It is not necessary to write something in relation to every area; just write down things about the areas that seem relevant or important to you.

Increasing your understanding of yourself

i) Reconciling the past – how are your past experiences related to your current situation?

_____

_____

_____

_____

ii) Increasing awareness of yourself – what are the important things that you have learnt about yourself?

_____
_____
_____
_____

iii) Acknowledging the impact of mental distress on yourself – how do stress and emotional problems affect you?

_____
_____
_____
_____

iv) Acknowledging the effects of psychiatric treatment – what effects do the mental health system and psychiatric treatment have on you?

_____
_____
_____
_____

v) Making sense of your experiences of mental distress – how do you understand what has happened to you?

_____
_____
_____
_____

Empowering yourself

i) Seeking knowledge – what can you do to find out more about your difficulties?

_____
_____
_____
_____

ii) Taking control – what could you do to take more control of your life or treatment?

_____

_____

_____

_____

iii) Self-motivation – how can you increase your motivation?

_____

_____

_____

_____

iv) Self-esteem – how could you improve or maintain your self-esteem?

_____

_____

_____

_____

v)   Sharing and validating experiences – what could you do to allow you to share your experiences with people whom you trust, or with people who have gone through similar difficulties?

_____

_____

_____

_____

Rebuilding of social support

i)   Key worker relationship – do you have a key worker or care coordinator? Do you get on with your key worker? What would you like from your key worker?

_____

_____

_____

_____

ii) Developing social relationships/networks – what could you do to see more people or make new friends?

_____

_____

_____

_____

iii) Developing family support – do you have a family? Are there things that they can do to help you?

_____

_____

_____

_____

iv) Accessing independent support – are there any sources of support from elsewhere that you could make use of?

_____

_____

_____

_____

Rebuilding life skills and independence – the importance of active participation in life

i) Actively engaging with life – what could you do in order to make your life more interesting or varied? Could you develop any new hobbies or interests?

_____

_____

_____

_____

ii) Taking risks – are there any things that you've wanted to do, but been too worried about to attempt?

_____

_____

_____

_____

iii) Creating a sense of purpose in life – how do you (or could you) make life feel more meaningful?

_____

_____

_____

_____

iv) Importance of voluntary work and employment – are there any oppor-
tunities for work that you could make use of?

_____
_____
_____
_____

Recovery as a process of change

i) Personal transformation and change – how have you changed for the
better as a result of your experiences?

_____
_____
_____
_____

ii) Challenging the self – what could you do to challenge any negative views
that you have of yourself?

_____
_____
_____
_____

iii) Changing attitudes – what could you do to try to change other people's
attitudes towards people with mental health difficulties?

_____
_____
_____
_____

iv) What changes would you like to see in mental health services in relation to
recovery? Could you discuss these with someone (such as a therapist or
key worker)?

_____
_____
_____
_____

By thinking about these areas, and making use of the strategies that you
have learnt throughout this book, you will hopefully be able to live out
your own successful story of recovery. Of course, you are likely to
encounter some setbacks at times. Like almost everyone, you may also

experience occasional periods of severe stress. At difficult moments, it may help to remember that recovery is a journey without a clear ending. Of course, the same is true of much of life in general – except perhaps at the extreme limits of old age, there are always more goals to aim for, and new experiences that can be sought out and enjoyed.

We wish you good luck on your personal journey and hope that this book is helpful in keeping you on a path that suits you (a bit like a road map). The final chapter, which follows, describes some people and organizations that might help on your road to recovery.

Who can help?

As discussed in the last chapter, cognitive therapy can be a powerful tool to help on the journey to recovery, but there are many other things that can also contribute. In this final chapter we will discuss the range of people who may be available to help you with different aspects of your recovery journey. There are a number of different groups of people that you could consider seeking help from, for example family and friends, voluntary organizations, self-help groups, services within the National Health Service if you live in the UK, or equivalent mental health services if you live elsewhere. It also may be possible to get help from private practitioners, for example by paying for specific psychological therapies, which may not be readily available within your area.

Ideally, the most important of these groups would be friends and family. However, many people with psychosis lose contact with many of their friends and family members, often because their psychotic experiences prevent them from keeping in touch. It is, therefore, possible that you have become isolated and have limited contact with other people and that some of the positive symptoms of psychosis could have contributed to this. You may have felt that you could not trust other people, your experiences may have become worse when in the company of others or you may have felt that other people would not want to spend time with you.

On the other hand, some of the negative symptoms associated with psychosis can also affect the ability to maintain social relationships. For example, some people find that they have little motivation or interest in keeping up with friends. If this has been your experience, then hopefully some of the strategies discussed throughout this book may have helped. It may now be time to attempt to rekindle some of the friendships that you may have let slip over time, or to contact family members who you have not seen much of lately. Perhaps it is time to think about trying to develop a new network of friends.

Hopefully someone working in the mental health field, for example a clinical psychologist, nurse, social worker or your doctor, will have directed you to this book and they will have gone through the material in the various chapters with you. If this is the case, then this person is obviously someone you could consider seeking more help from.

Constructing a list of people who you could turn to for assistance could be useful. The list could include the sort of help that these people might offer and should be as long and inclusive as possible. It could also include people who might offer help not just to you, but also to your friends or family, for example by helping them to understand some of your difficulties. It may be helpful to talk to any professionals involved with your care about the kind of help they expect to be able to offer now and in the future and how they will be able to respond to any future crises. You may already have a care plan agreed with the professionals and it would be useful for you to know what this says and to ensure that it adequately describes your needs. You may also wish to make something called an advance directive, which states how you would like to be treated if you become unwell in the future.

Let us now briefly look at the kinds of people who might be involved in your care.

The case manager or care coordinator

A case manager is a mental health worker who is meant to have a caseload of around 15–25 people, and who sees these people on a regular basis in order to coordinate the various aspects of care that they require. A case manager could be from any discipline, for example nursing, social work, psychiatry or clinical psychology, although most commonly they are nurses, social workers and occupational therapists. Some case managers may also provide services directly, for example by giving prescribed medication or by helping people fill in applications for benefits.

The cognitive behavioural therapist

A cognitive therapist or cognitive behavioural therapist will use many of the strategies outlined throughout this book. They should be specially trained in the use of these strategies and have regular supervision from someone who has more experience of providing this form of therapy. As you will by now be aware, this therapy highlights the way in which we think about events and how these thoughts affect our moods and behaviour. A therapist using CBT will then help you evaluate whether these thoughts are accurate reflections of the available evidence, or whether there might be alternative interpretations of your experience that are worth considering. CBT therapists may come from any discipline, but in the UK they are very often clinical psychologists or psychiatric nurses.

The community psychiatric nurse (CPN)

A CPN is a registered mental health nurse who works in the community but who often has some experience of working on psychiatric wards. A CPN may dispense medication (including giving depot injections), assess patients' difficulties, monitor their progress and provide some forms of psychological therapy, although they vary quite a lot in the extent to which they are able to do each of these things. Many CPNs will be aware of the strategies discussed within this book, although not many will have undergone specific training in cognitive behaviour therapy.

The counsellor

A counsellor is someone who listens to problems and has a very non-directive way of helping. Typically, a counsellor will provide emotional support and will help patients to understand their problems but will not use the kind of specific strategies employed by a cognitive behavioural therapist. A warm supportive relationship of this sort is often helpful, but counselling appears not to be as effective with psychotic problems as CBT. For this reason, counselling is usually reserved for people who have life crises or less severe difficulties.

The general practitioner (GP or family doctor)

Your GP will be responsible for your general physical health as well as some aspects of your mental health. However, they usually have limited expertise in the treatment of psychotic problems, so they will usually refer people with these kinds of difficulties on to specialist psychiatric services. Nonetheless, a good GP can play an important role in a patient's care once the specialist services have become involved, for example by keeping an eye on progress or by making sure that prescriptions are repeated.

The occupational therapist (OT)

Occupational therapists are trained to help people function effectively. In the mental health field, OTs are often concerned with the living skills of patients. People with psychosis sometimes lose the ability to interact effectively with other people, or even to look after themselves properly (in extreme cases, they may not be able to keep themselves clean, or cook for themselves). This usually happens after people have become isolated for a long time, and feel hopeless and inadequate as a consequence. An OT can play a vital role in helping the person recover lost living and social skills in these circumstances. Some OTs also help in other ways, for example by acting as case managers, and some have acquired skills in specific psychological therapies such as CBT.

The pharmacist

Pharmacists are experts in the use of medication. Although they do not prescribe drugs directly to patients, they advise doctors about the safety and effectiveness of different kinds of medication. They have extensive knowledge about the side effects of different drugs and how different medications interact with each other. Although you are most likely to meet a pharmacist when getting your drugs from your local pharmacy, some work as specialist psychiatric pharmacists, mainly in psychiatric hospitals.

It has been said that pharmacy is perhaps the least appreciated and least effectively utilized of the health care professions. Recently, some pharmacists have begun to work directly with patients, providing them with detailed information about their medical treatment. If you are being prescribed psychiatric drugs and you are offered the chance to meet with a pharmacist to receive advice about how best to take your treatment and how you are likely to be affected by it, it would almost certainly be a good idea to make use of this opportunity.

The psychiatrist

The psychiatrist is a medical doctor who specializes in the diagnosis and treatment of psychiatric problems. In most circumstances, medical doctors are the only people who are allowed to prescribe drugs (although this may change, with nurses and perhaps some other professionals being allowed to prescribe in very limited circumstances). They will, therefore, take overall responsibility for any medical treatment of your problems. Psychiatrists also assess patients to see whether they are getting better, and are involved in decisions to admit people to hospital when it is against their will. Following the model of physical medicine, psychiatrists often see their patients infrequently unless they are in hospital, and will focus on reviewing progress and adjusting any medical treatment accordingly. However, a few also find the time to practise psychological treatments.

The clinical psychologist

Most clinical psychologists qualify with a doctorate in psychology, so although they may be entitled to call themselves 'Dr', they should not be confused with medical doctors and (except in a small number of states in the USA) cannot prescribe drugs. Instead, they use psychological treatments to help their patients understand and manage their difficulties. Clinical psychologists usually begin by collecting a wide variety of information to reach a psychological 'formulation' (an account of a person's problems and how those problems developed), which makes sense to the patient. This may require a number of sessions (meetings). The formulation is then used to plan psychological treatment, which is very often cognitive behaviour therapy. For any psychological treatment to be effective there has to be a warm and collaborative relationship between the psychologist and the patient. Courses of psychological treatment vary in duration, but typically require weekly meetings over a period of six months or so.

The social worker

A social worker is someone who works with people to achieve positive change in the context of their families and communities. In mental health, social workers can be involved alongside medical doctors in the decision to admit patients to hospital. However, social workers often see themselves as patient-advocates, protecting their patients' rights. Social workers frequently act as case managers in mental health teams. They may also provide help and support about a range of practical issues, including housing and benefits.

Many or all of these professionals may be involved with your care. As we have already indicated, you may also be able to obtain help from voluntary or self-help groups. There is a wide range of non-statutory organizations that try to offer assistance to people with mental health difficulties and access to these will vary in different parts of the country. However, in the UK there are some national organizations, which will be briefly reviewed here.

Hearing Voices Network

The Hearing Voices Network is an excellent organization that is committed to helping people who hear voices. The aims of the network are to raise awareness of voice hearing, visions, tactile sensations and other unusual experiences; to give men, women and children who have these experiences an opportunity to talk freely about this together; and to support anyone with these experiences seeking to understand, learn and grow from them in their own way. They run a number of self-help groups around the country, and also offer training sessions about voices to mental health workers and the general public. They also provide a telephone service that provides information about voices, and publish a newsletter four times a year. The Hearing Voices Network can be contacted at their website, which is listed below.

MIND

MIND describes itself as 'the leading mental health charity in England and Wales'. Its stated aims are to create a better life for everyone who experiences mental health problems by advancing their views, needs and ambitions; by challenging discrimination and promoting inclusion; by influencing government policy through campaigning and education; and by inspiring the development of quality services that reflect patients' needs. MIND runs regular conferences and training events for people with mental health problems and their families. MIND can be contacted at their website, which is listed below.

Rethink

Rethink is the new operating name for the organization that used to be known as the National Schizophrenia Fellowship. At the time of writing, it is the largest severe mental illness charity in the UK. Rethink are dedicated to improving the lives of everyone affected by severe mental illness, whether they have a condition themselves or care for others who do. They provide a wide range of community services, including employment projects, supported housing, day services, helplines, residential care and respite centres. All of their services try to help people take more control of their own lives by building their confidence and strengthening their skills. Rethink can be contacted at their website, which is listed below.

The National Institute for Mental Health in England

NIMHE was launched in June 2002. It is an organization funded by the UK Department of Health and aims to improve the quality of life for people of all ages who experience mental distress. Working beyond the National Health Service and through local development centres, one of its main aims is to support staff who wish to develop and introduce innovations in mental health care. NIMHE can be contacted at their website, which is listed below.

SANE

SANE was established in 1986 in response to public concern about the care of people with mental health problems, which was stimulated by a series of newspaper articles written by Marjorie Wallace, now SANE's chief executive. The articles highlighted the neglect of people suffering from psychosis and the poor services available. SANE's main objectives are: to raise awareness and respect for people with mental health problems and their families; to improve the education and training of mental health professionals, and thereby secure better services; to undertake research into the causes of serious mental illness through The Prince of Wales International Centre for SANE Research; and to provide information and emotional support to those experiencing mental health problems, their families and carers through a telephone service known as SANELINE. SANE can be contacted at their website, which is listed below.

A final source of potential support and information is the Internet, although it is important to note that, as anyone can set up an Internet site and there is no quality control, some sites may provide information that is unhelpful or misleading. However, many of the national organizations mentioned have websites that are very reliable, some of which provide excellent material to help people understand some of the difficulties they are experiencing. Below is a list of useful Internet sites, some of which provide not only information but also message boards or facilities to post questions. In some cases, these sites will allow you to get support from people who may have been through similar experiences. There are also websites designed to administer self-guided cognitive behaviour therapy for emotional problems such as anxiety and depression. While this list was up to date at the time of publishing, the Internet develops at a very fast pace and it is possible that these addresses may change in future.

Department of Health   http://www.dh.gov.uk
Rethink   http://www.rethink.org.uk
NIMHE   http://www.nimhe.csip.org.uk
SANE   http://www.sane.org.uk
NHS Direct   http://www.nhsdirect.nhs.uk
BABCP   http://www.babcp.org.uk
Hearing Voices Network   http://www.hearing-voices.org
MIND   http://www.mind.org.uk
Mood gym   http://www.moodgym.anu.edu.au

When seeking help, look for people who are actually supportive. Some-times people have dogmatic opinions about what we should do. Although their advice may be helpful, a badgering or cajoling attitude is usually off-putting. Try to identify those people in your social network (and in health services) who are prepared to take some time to listen to what your problems are and then discuss with you all the different options that might be available.

References

1. Bentall, R.P. (2003) *Madness explained: psychosis and human nature*. London: Penguin Books Ltd.
2. Strauss, J.S. (1969) Hallucinations and delusions as points on continua function: Rating scale evidence. *Archives of General Psychiatry*, 21: 581–586.
3. Grimby, A. (1993) Bereavement among elderly people: Grief reactions, post-bereavement hallucinations and quality of life. *Acta Psychiatrica Scandinavica*, 87: 72–80.
4. Tien, A.Y. (1991) Distribution of hallucinations in the population. *Social Psychiatry and Psychiatric Epidemiology*, 26: 287–292.
5. Posey, T.B. and M.E. Losch (1983) Auditory hallucinations of hearing voices in 375 normal subjects. *Imagination, Cognition and Personality*, 2: 99–113.
6. Romme, M. and A. Escher (1989) Hearing voices. *Schizophrenia Bulletin*, 15: 209–216.
7. Kingdon, D.G. and D. Turkington (1994) *Cognitive-behavioural therapy of schizophrenia*. Hove: Lawrence Erlbaum.
8. McGuire, P.K., D.A. Silbersweig, I. Wright and R.M. Murray (1996) The neural correlates of inner speech and auditory verbal imagery in schizophrenia: Relationship to auditory verbal hallucinations. *British Journal of Psychiatry*, 169: 148–159.
9. Verdoux, H., S. Maurice-Tison, B. Gay, J. Van Os, R. Salamon and M.L. Bourgeois (1998) A survey of delusional ideation in primary-care patients. *Psychological Medicine*, 28: 127–134.
10. Cox, D. and P. Cowling (1989) *Are you normal?* London: Tower Press.
11. Peters, E.R., S.A. Joseph and P.A. Garety (1999) Measurement of delusional ideation in the normal population: Introducing the PDI (Peters et al. Delusions Inventory). *Schizophrenia Bulletin*, 25: 553–576.
12. Garety, P.A. and D.R. Hemsley (1994) *Delusions*. London: Psychology Press.
13. Huq, S.F., P.A. Garety and D.R. Hemsley (1988) Probabilistic judgements in deluded and nondeluded subjects. *Quarterly Journal of Experimental Psychology*, 40A: 801–812.
14. Bentall, R.P., R. Corcoran, R. Howard, R. Blackwood and P. Kinderman (2001) Persecutory delusions: A review and theoretical integration. *Clinical Psychology Review*, 22: 1–50.
15. Peters, E., S. Day, J. McKenna and G. Orbach (1999) Delusional ideation in religious and psychotic populations. *British Journal of Clinical Psychology*, 38: 83–96.
16. Kraepelin, E. (1919/1973) *Dementia preacox and paraphrenia*. Huntington, NY: Kriger.
17. Beck, A.T. (1976) *Cognitive therapy and the emotional disorders*. New York: International Universities Press.
18. Morrison, A.P. (2001) The interpretation of intrusions in psychosis: An integrative cognitive approach to hallucinations and delusions. *Behavioural and Cognitive Psychotherapy*, 29: 257–276.
19. Morrison, A.P., J.C. Renton, H. Dunn, S. Williams and R.P. Bentall (2003) *Cognitive therapy for psychosis: a formulation-based approach*. London: Psychology Press.

20. Greenberger, D. and C.A. Padesky (1995) *Mind over mood: a cognitive therapy treatment manual for clients*. New York: Guilford Press.
21. Beck, A.T., A.J. Rush, B.F. Shaw and G. Emery (1979) *Cognitive therapy of depression*. New York: Guilford Press.
22. Salkovskis, P.M. (1991) The importance of behaviour in the maintenance of anxiety and panic: A cognitive account. *Behavioural Psychotherapy*, 19: 6–19.
23. Wells, A. (1997) *Cognitive therapy for anxiety disorders*. London: Wiley.
24. Clark, D.M. (1999) Anxiety disorders: why they persist and how to treat them. *Behaviour Research and Therapy*, 37: 5–27.
25. Tarrier, N. (2002) Coping strategies and self-regulation in the treatment of psychosis. In A.P. Morrison (ed.) *A case book of cognitive therapy*. Hove: Brunner-Routledge.
26. Henquet, C., L. Krabbendam, J. Spauwen, C. Kaplan, R. Lieb, H.U. Wittchen and J. van Os (2005) Prospective cohort study of cannabis use, predisposition for psychosis, and psychotic symptoms in young people. *British Medical Journal*, 330: 11.
27. Gumley, A., C.A. White and K. Power (1999) An interacting cognitive subsystems model of relapse and the course of psychosis. *Clinical Psychology and Psychotherapy*, 6: 261–278.
28. Birchwood, M., J. Smith, F. Macmillan, B. Hogg, R. Prasad, C. Harvey and S. Bering (1989) Predicting relapse in schizophrenia: The development and implementation of an early signs monitoring system using patients and families as observers. *Psychological Medicine*, 19: 649–656.
29. Herz, M.I. and C. Melville (1980) Relapse in schizophrenia. *American Journal of Psychiatry*, 127: 801–812.
30. Gumley, A.I., M. O'Grady, L. McNay, J. Reilly, K. Power and J. Norrie (2003) Early intervention for relapse in schizophrenia: results of a 12-month randomised controlled trial of cognitive behaviour therapy. *Psychological Medicine*, 33: 419–431.
31. Healy, D. (2005) *Psychiatric drugs explained*, 5th edn. London: Elsevier.
32. Pitt, L., M. Kilbride, S. Nothard, M. Welford and A.P. Morrison (2007) Researching recovery from psychosis: A user-led project. *Psychiatric Bulletin*, 31: 55–60.

Appendix

HOW AM I FEELING?

Event: (What am I doing? Who am I with?)

Feeling: (What emotion am I experiencing?)

How strong is this feeling?

0   10   20   30   40   50   60   70   80   90   100

IDENTIFYING AUTOMATIC THOUGHTS

Event	Thoughts	Feeling	Behaviour
What happened?	What was going through your mind? What are you worrying is the worst that might happen? What images or memories come to mind in this situation?	What were you feeling? How strong was it 0–100?	What did you do?

EVALUATING AUTOMATIC THOUGHTS

Thought:	Belief conviction: Anxiety:
Evidence supporting the thought	**Evidence NOT supporting the thought**

How much do you believe in the thought now?
How anxious are you now?
Do you think this was a fact or just a thought?
Is there another possible explanation for this experience?

EVALUATING BELIEFS ABOUT VOICES

Belief about voices:	Belief conviction: Anxiety:
Evidence supporting the belief	**Evidence NOT supporting the belief**
How much do you believe this now? *How anxious are you now?* *Is there another possible explanation for this experience?*	

EVALUATING WHAT THE VOICES SAY

What the voices say:	Belief conviction: Anxiety:
Evidence supporting the voices	**Evidence NOT supporting the voices**

How much do you believe this now?
How anxious are you now?
Do you think this was a fact?
Is there a more accurate statement that reflects the truth?

EVIDENCE LIST FOR DIFFERENT EXPLANATIONS

Interpretation	Evidence for	Evidence against	Belief %	Associated feeling %

SUMMARIZING EVIDENCE TOWARDS A BALANCED THOUGHT

Summary of evidence supporting the automatic thought	Summary of evidence **NOT** supporting the automatic thought
The balanced view:	

Belief in the balanced thought:
Belief in the anxious thought:
Anxiety now:

WEIGHING UP BENEFITS AND PROBLEMS

Benefits of trying this approach	Problems with trying this approach

BEHAVIOURAL EXPERIMENTS FORM

Thought to be tested:

Belief in thought: (0–100%) Before experiment

			After experiment		
Experiment to test thought	Likely problems	Strategies to deal with problems	Expected outcome	Actual outcome	Alternative thought

EVALUATING COPING STRATEGIES

What do you do to cope?	Helpful aspects of this strategy	Unhelpful aspects of this strategy	Is there an alternative?

'OLD' CORE BELIEF WORKSHEET

Core belief to be tested _____

Write below any evidence that suggests that this core belief is not 100% true at all times. Has someone said or done something that does not fit with your core belief?
Has someone said or done something that suggests that they do not agree with your core belief? Is there anyone who would point out things that do not fit with your core belief? What would they point out?

1.	
2.	
3.	
4.	
5.	
6.	
7.	

'NEW' CORE BELIEF WORKSHEET

New or 'alternative' belief _____

Write below any evidence that suggests that this new belief is true. Has someone said or done something that fits with this new belief or shows they agree with it? Is there anyone who would point out things that fit with your new core belief? What would they point out?

1.	
2.	
3.	
4.	
5.	
6.	
7.	

FORMULATION

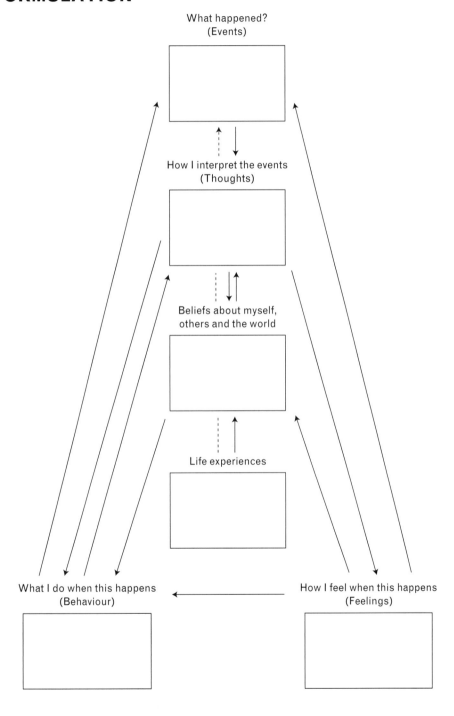

What happened?
(Events)

How I interpret the events
(Thoughts)

Beliefs about myself,
others and the world

Life experiences

What I do when this happens
(Behaviour)

How I feel when this happens
(Feelings)

Index